Learn Spanish for Beginners, Dummies & Idiots

By Giovanni Rigters

© Copyright 2021 - All rights reserved.

The content contained within this book may not be reproduced, duplicated or transmitted without direct written permission from the author or the publisher.

Under no circumstances will any blame or legal responsibility be held against the publisher, or author, for any damages, reparation, or monetary loss due to the information contained within this book, either directly or indirectly.

Legal Notice:

This book is copyright protected. It is only for personal use. You cannot amend, distribute, sell, use, quote or paraphrase any part, or the content within this book, without the consent of the author or publisher.

Disclaimer Notice:

Please note the information contained within this document is for educational and entertainment purposes only. All effort has been executed to present accurate, up to date, reliable, complete information. No warranties of any kind are declared or implied. Readers acknowledge that the author is not engaging in the rendering of legal, financial, medical or professional advice. The content within this book has been derived from various sources. Please consult a licensed professional before attempting any techniques outlined in this book.

By reading this document, the reader agrees that under no circumstances is the author responsible for any losses, direct or indirect, that are incurred as a result of the use of information contained within this document, including, but not limited to, errors, omissions, or inaccuracies.

Table Of Contents

Introduction

Chapter 1: Basic Grammar

Gender Matters

Opening Punctuation

Strong Syllables and Diacritic Acute

Numbers

Articles

Adjectives

Adverbs

Chapter 2: Pronunciation

Alphabet

Particular Sounds

Syllable Changes

Chapter 3: Nouns & Pronouns

Nouns

Personal Pronouns

Possessive Pronouns

Reflexive Pronouns

Interrogative Pronouns

Relative Pronouns

Demostrative Pronouns
Indefinite Pronouns

Chapter 4: Verbs
Impersonal Verb Conjugations
Regular Verb Conjugation
Irregular Verb Conjugation
Verb To Be
Verb To Do
Verb To Have

Chapter 5: Basic Sentence Construction
Affirmative Sentences
Negative Sentences
Interrogative Sentences

Chapter 6: Time Tenses
Verbal Moods
Indicative Tense

Chapter 7: Dates and Time
Days of the Week
Months of the Year
Moments of the Day
Telling the Time

Chapter 8: Greetings & Simple Conversations

Greetings

Presenting Yourself

Asking Someone to Present Himself

Asking Someone About Themselves

Talking About Yourself

Asking Someone About How He Is

Telling Someone About How You Are

Asking for Directions

Giving Directions

Asking for the Day and Time

Conclusion

Introduction

Often in Spanish lessons, students maintain that they're far better at Spanish than they really are. These students saw a couple of Spanish lessons, maybe they memorized a Spanish traveler's guide, and perhaps they've even maintained simple conversations with Spanish speakers and were able to make themselves understood.

However, when you look at how they write and speak in Spanish, you realize that they're making plenty of mistakes, especially in verb conjugation and pronunciation. This happens because they don't have a good foundation in grammar, so they don't really understand how Spanish works, even if they're able to convey an idea or two in the right context. If you want to avoid being this kind of student, this book is the right place for you.

Spanish is one of the most important languages in the world. There are over 463 million native Spanish speakers in the world, so it's quite possible that if you want to sell a product, work for an international firm, or just travel through many beautiful and interesting places, you must be able to communicate in Spanish.

It's no wonder you're interested in learning this language, but it's also true that learning Spanish isn't a walk in the park for native English speaker. Spanish verb conjugation and pronunciation is difficult to learn for the average native English speakers. It requires relentless application from the student, but pure effort doesn't get you far without the right teaching method, which is why it's so scary to look for a new learning path for this beautiful language.

This intricate situation is where this book comes in. This book provides a proven Spanish-learning method that focuses heavily on grammar and the Spanish language. By learning the foundations of Spanish and its fundamental differences with English, everything else comes much more easily.

This book follows a step-by-step learning process where you'll get from the easier and most fundamental parts of the Spanish language to the more complex bits of information. You won't have to worry about making rookie mistakes in Spanish conversations as you won't just be able to understand what everyone else is saying, you'll also know exactly why they're saying it that way and the correct way to answer.

Your Spanish learning path takes form in the following chapters with grammar concepts, common words, usual phrases you'll use in everyday conversations, and examples. Everything is followed by the translation and pronunciation, so you can learn how to speak Spanish while you learn the fundamentals of the language. By following the chapters step by step, paying attention to every part, and making the conscious effort to learn and remember each step, you'll be able to have conversations in Spanish, read, and write in the

Spanish language. The rest will come with the experience that allows you to expand your vocabulary, but the harder part, the fundamental grammar concepts, will be already earned in your mind.

Learning Spanish may be hard, and it's certainly a long process, but the reward is worth the effort. Once you know that you'll be putting your effort into a trustworthy learning path, the only thing left for you to do is to move on to the first chapter and start learning. It will all be worth it once you've gone through the book and you're finally able to communicate correctly in Spanish.

Chapter 1: Basic Grammar

There's a couple of fundamental differences between English and Spanish that you must start with if you wish to learn how to speak Spanish. These are concepts that affect the whole language. Once we've got this covered, we'll go over various types of words and Spanish grammar concepts.

Gender Matters

Spanish makes a distinction between masculine and feminine in the language. Unlike English, which is a gender-neutral language, Spanish applies genders to every noun that appears in each sentence, no matter if it's a person or an inanimate object. The gender of a noun often affects the noun, but it also affects the words that are around it, so it's possible to know the gender of a noun just by paying attention to these words and the pronunciation of the noun.

The words that change with the gender of the noun are the articles, adjectives, and participle verbs; articles and adjectives will be covered in this chapter, while participle verbs will be covered in the third chapter.

Noun Pronunciation

There are two main situations regarding noun pronunciation and gender in Spanish. Nouns can be either feminine or masculine depending on whether they end with "a" (feminine) or "o" (masculine), and nouns that are always feminine or masculine no matter the context where they're used. The first nouns are usually animals and groups of persons but without the names.

For example, if you want to speak about a female cat in Spanish, you'll say "gata" (pronounced gah-tah), and for a male cat, you'll say "gato" (pronounced gah-toh); if you want to talk about a girl, you'll say "niña" (nee-neeah), but you'll say "niño" (nee-neeoh) when talking about a boy. Notice how feminine nouns end with "a" and masculine nouns end with "o". This isn't the case every time, but it's the case with these types of nouns.

The second type of noun is stable, but in its stability, it has its own gender. Staying with the animals as an example, if we were to talk about an alligator, we'd say "lagarto" (lah-gahr-toh); it's a masculine noun in pronunciation, and it stays that way whether it's in reference to a male or a female alligator. An example of a feminine pronunciation is whale, "ballena" (bah-yeh-nah), it's feminine and is pronounced that way no matter if it's in reference to a male or female whale.

There are also some nouns that are stable in their pronunciation, but the accompanying words can change depending on the gender of the object referenced. This is the case for professions, so if you want to talk about a male dentist "dentista" (dehn-tees-tah), it's pronounced the same way when we talk about a female dentist (also "dentista").

Opening Punctuation

Punctuation marks in Spanish work the same way they do in English with two fundamental differences: exclamation marks and interrogation marks (question marks). In English, if you want to ask a question or make an exclamation, all you need to do is use an interrogation mark (?) or exclamation mark (!) at the end of the sentence.

This isn't enough in Spanish, where an opening exclamation and/or interrogation mark ("¡" and "¿" respectively) are used at the beginning of the sentence to mark the beginning of the interrogative sentence or the exclamation sentence. This allows Spanish users to make a question of less than a conventional sentence, or an exclamation of even one word, without needing to rely on the context as it happens with English.

Strong Syllables and Diacritic Acute

Words in Spanish sometimes carry a symbol called a "tilde" (teel-deh) over their strong syllables. When you see this symbol (called a diacritic acute in English), you'll know that in the particular pronunciation of that word, the syllable with a diacritic acute is always the strong syllable of the word. However, since not every word carries a diacritic acute, it's necessary to learn the rules behind placing these "tildes" in order to write Spanish properly.

The "tilde" is used mainly to trace the difference between words that are written the same way, but they have different meanings depending on the context. These particular cases will be often explored and studied in this book, but it's not the only relevant aspect of tildes in Spanish. The easiest and most common rules behind tildes are dependent on Spanish word classification regarding their strong syllables.

"Agudas" or Acute Words

A Spanish word will be "aguda" if its last syllable is the strongest syllable of the word. Agudas always have a tilde when they end with a vowel, an "n", or an "s" when the "n" or "s" are preceded by a vowel. If neither of these conditions is true, the word is written without a tilde. We'll see some examples of agudas with their translation, pronunciation, and diacritic acute placement.

Spanish	**Pronunciation**	**English**
Canción	Can-seeohn	Song

Café	Cah-feh	Coffee
Natural	Nah-too-rahl	Natural
Integridad	Een-teh-gree-dahd	Integrity

"Llanas" or "Graves" Words

These are the words that place their strong syllable in the second to last syllable. They can be translated as "flat" and "grave" words respectively, and their rules regarding tilde placement are the complete opposite of the rules for acute words. Therefore, flat words never have a tilde when they end with a vowel, or if they end with a vowel followed by the consonants "n" or "s".

This means that flat words that end with any other consonant always have a tilde, and they also have a tilde if they end with "n" or "s" in particular when these aren't preceded by a vowel.

An important conclusion you'll get once you understand both acute and flat words is how to pronounce these words just by reading them. Of course, if the word has a tilde, you'll know which syllable is the strong one. Now, if there's no tilde, all you need to do is look at the end of the word to figure out if it's an acute or flat word. If there's no tilde, and the word ends with a vowel, "n", or "s" preceded by vowels, then you know it's a flat word. If the opposite is true, then it's an acute word. Here are some examples of flat words.

Spanish	Pronunciation	English
Árbol	Ahr-bohl	Tree
Lápiz	Lah-pees	Pencil
Colmillo	Cohl-mee-yoh	Fang
Nube	Noo-beh	Cloud

"Esdrújulas"

The easiest group to learn, esdrújulas are words that place their strong syllable in the third to last syllable (one step before the flat words). This group of words always has a tilde, so if you read one of these words, you'll always know it's an esdrújula, and if you hear one of these words, you'll know that it must be written with a tilde.

The same thing happens with words called "sobreesdrújulas", which have the same rule of always carrying a tilde, but the strong syllable is even before it would be in esdrújulas.

Spanish	Pronunciation	English
Lógico	Loh-hee-coh	Logic
Pájaro	Pah-hah-roh	Bird

Ábremelo	Ah-breh-meh-loh	Open it for me
Cómanselo	Coh-mahn-seh-loh	Eat it

Numbers

Spanish numbers follow a very similar pattern as English numbers, so it isn't hard to learn them. Once the pattern is understood, it's possible to know how to read all numbers in Spanish just by looking at their symbolic representation. Once each step of the numbering pattern is set, we'll start skipping numbers only to show those that are necessary.

Cardinal Numbers

Most cardinal numbers aren't affected by the gender of the object they're counting, but not all of them. One, as well as numbers that end with one, and numbers in the hundreds are, instead, affected by gender, and they can end with O as the last vowel for masculine or mixed groups, or A as the last vowel for feminine groups.

Number	**Cardinal Writing**	**Pronunciation**
0	Cero	Seh-roh

1	Uno	Oo-noh
2	Dos	Dohs
3	Tres	Trehs
4	Cuatro	Cooah-troh
5	Cinco	Seen-coh
6	Seis	Seh_ees
7	Siete	See_eh-teh
8	Ocho	Oh-choh
9	Nueve	Nooeh-beh
10	Diez	Dee_ehs
11	Once	Ohn-se
12	Doce	Doh-se
13	Trece	Treh-seh
14	Catorce	Cah-tohr-seh
15	Quince	Keen-seh
16	Dieciséis	Dee_eh-see-seh_ees
17	Diecisiete	Deeh_eh-see-see_eh-teh
18	Dieciocho	Dee_eh-seeoh-

		choh
19	Diecinueve	Dee_eh-see-nooeh-beh
20	Veinte	Beh_een-teh
21	Veintiuno	Beh_een-teeoo-noh
22	Veintidós	Beh_een-tee-dohs
23	Veintitrés	Beh_een-tee-trehs
24	Veinticuatro	Beh_een-tee-cooah-troh
25	Veinticinco	Beh_een-tee-seen-co
26	Veintiséis	Beh_een-tee-seh_ees
27	Veintisiete	Beh_een-tee-see_eh-teh
28	Veintiocho	Beh_een-teeoh-choh
29	Veintinueve	Beh_een-tee-nooeh-beh
30	Treinta	Treh_een-tah

31	Treinta y uno	Treh_een-tah ee oo-noh
32	Treinta y dos	Treh_een-tah ee dohs
33	Treinta y tres	Tre_een-tah ee trehs
34	Treinta y cuatro	Tre_een-tah ee cooah-troh
35	Treinta y cinco	Tre_een-tah ee seen-coh
36	Treinta y seis	Treh_een-tah ee seh_ees
37	Treinta y siete	Treh_een-tah ee see_eh-teh
38	Treinta y ocho	Treh_een-tah ee oh-choh
39	Treinta y nueve	Treh_een-tah ee nooeh-beh
40	Cuarenta	Cooah-rehn-tah
41	Cuarenta y uno	Cooah-rehn-tah ee oo-noh
50	Cincuenta	Seen-cooehn-tah
60	Sesenta	Seh-sehn-tah

70	Setenta	Seh-tehn-tah
80	Ochenta	Oh-chehn-tah
90	Noventa	Noh-behn-tah
100	Cien	See_ehn
200	Doscientos	Dohs-see_ehn-tohs
300	Trescientos	Trehs-see_ehn-tohs
400	Cuatrocientos	Cooah-troh-see_ehn-tohs
500	Quinientos	Kee-nee_ehn-tohs
600	Seiscientos	Seh_ees-see_ehn-tohs
700	Setecientos	Seh-teh-see_ehn-tohs
800	Ochocientos	Oh-choh-see_ehn-tohs
900	Novecientos	Noh-beh-see_ehn-tohs
1000	Mil	Meel
1.500	Mil quinientos	Meel kee-nee_ehn-tohs

5.000	Cinco mil	Seen-coh meel
10.000	Diez mil	Dee_ehs meel
50.000	Cincuenta mil	Seen-cooehn-tah meel
100.000	Cien mil	See_ehn meel
101.000	Ciento un mil	See_ehn-toh oon meel
150.000	Ciento cincuenta mil	See_ehn-toh seen-cooehn-tah meel
500.000	Quinientos mil	Kee-nee_ehn-tohs meel
1.000.000	Un millón	Oon mee-yohn
1.500.000	Un millón quinientos mil	Oon mee-yohn kee-nee_ehn-tohs meel
10.000.000	Diez millones	Dee_ehs mee-yoh-nehs

Ordinal Numbers

Unlike Spanish cardinal numbers, Spanish ordinal numbers are all affected by gender. Therefore, they can either have O as their last vowel when they're counting a masculine object, or A when it's a feminine object.

Number	Ordinal Writing	Pronunciation
1	Primero	Pree-meh-roh
2	Segundo	Seh-goon-doh
3	Tercero	Tehr-seh-roh
4	Cuarto	Cooahr-toh
5	Quinto	Keen-toh
6	Sexto	Sex-toh
7	Séptimo	Sep-tee-moh
8	Octavo	Ohc-tah-boh
9	Noveno	Noh-beh-noh
10	Décimo	Deh-see-moh
11	Undécimo	Oon-deh-see-moh
12	Duodécimo	Doo_oh-deh-see-moh
13	Decimotercero	Deh-see-moh-tehr-seh-roh
14	Decimocuarto	Deh-see-moh-

		cooahr-toh
15	Decimoquinto	Deh-see-moh-keen-toh
16	Decimosexto	Deh-see-moh-sex-toh
17	Decimoséptimo	Deh-see-moh-sep-tee-moh
18	Decimoctavo	Deh-see-moh-ohc-tah-boh
19	Decimonoveno	Deh-see-moh-noh-beh-noh
20	Vigésimo	Bee-heh-see-moh
21	Vigésimo primero / vigésimoprimero	Bee-heh-see-moh pree-meh-roh / bee-heh-see-moh-pree-meh-roh
22	Vigésimo segundo / vigésimosegundo	Bee-heh-see-moh seh-goon-doh / bee-heh-see-moh-seh-goon-doh
23	Vigésimo tercero / vigésimotercero	Bee-heh-see-moh tehr-seh-roh / bee-heh-

		see-moh-tehr-seh-roh
24	Vigésimo cuarto / vigésimocuarto	Bee-heh-see-moh cooahr-toh / bee-heh-see-moh-cooahr-toh
25	Vigésimo quinto / vigésimoquinto	Bee-heh-see-moh keen-toh / bee-heh-see-moh-keen-toh
26	Vigésimo sexto / vigésimosexto	Bee-heh-see-moh sex-toh / bee-heh-see-moh-sex-toh
27	Vigésimo séptimo / vigésimoséptimo	Bee-heh-see-moh sep-tee-moh / bee-heh-see-moh-sep-tee-moh
28	Vigésimo octavo / vigésimoctavo	Bee-heh-see-moh ohc-tah-boh / bee-heh-see-moh-ohc-tah-boh
29	Vigésimo noveno / vigésimonoveno	Bee-heh-see-moh noh-beh-noh / bee-heh-see-moh-noh-

		beh noh
30	Trigésimo	Tree-heh-see-moh
31	Trigésimo primero	Tree-heh-see-moh pree-meh-roh
32	Trigésimo segundo	Tree-heh-see-moh seh-goon-doh
33	Trigésimo tercero	Tree-heh-see-moh tehr-seh-roh
34	Trigésimo cuarto	Tree-heh-see-moh cooahr-toh
35	Trigésimo quinto	Tree-heh-see-moh keen-toh
36	Trigésimo sexto	Tree-heh-see-moh sex-toh
37	Trigésimo séptimo	Tree-heh-see-moh sep-tee-moh
38	Trigésimo octavo	Tree-heh-see-moh ohc-tah-boh

39	Trigésimo noveno	Tree-heh-see-moh noh-beh-noh
40	Cuadragésimo	Cooah-drah-heh-see-moh
41	Cuadragésimo primero	Cooah-drah-heh-see-moh pree-meh-roh
50	Quincuagésimo	Keen-cooah-heh-see-moh
60	Sexagésimo	Sex-sah-heh-see-moh
70	Septuagésimo	Sep-tooah-heh-see-moh
80	Octogésimo	Ohc-toh-heh-see-moh
90	Nonagésimo	Noh-nah-heh-see-moh
100	Centésimo	Sehn-teh-see-moh
200	Ducentésimo	Doo-sehn-teh-see-moh
300	Tricentésimo	Tree-sehn-teh-see-moh

400	Cuadringentésimo	Cooah-dreen-hen-teh-see-moh
500	Quingentésimo	Keen-hen-teh-see-moh
600	Sexcentésimo	Sex-sehn-teh-see-moh
700	Septingentésimo	Sep-teen-hen-teh-see-moh
800	Octingentésimo	Ohc-teen-hen-teh-see-moh
900	Noningentésimo	Noh-neen-gehn-teh-see-moh
1000	Milésimo	Mee-leh-see-moh
1.500	Milésimo quingentésimo	Mee-leh-see-moh keen-hen-teh-see-moh
5.000	Cincomilésimo	Seen-coh-mee-leh-see-moh
10.000	Diezmilésimo	Dee_ehs-mee-leh-see-moh
50.000	Cincuentamilésimo	Seen-cooehn-tah-mee-leh-

		see-moh
100.000	Cienmilésimo	See_ehn-mee-leh-see-moh
101.000	Ciento un milésimo	See_ehn-toh oon mee-leh-see-moh
150.000	Ciento cincuenta milésimo	See_ehn-toh seen-cooehn-tah mee-leh-see-moh
500.000	Quinientosmilésimo	Kee-nee_ehn-tohs-mee-leh-see-moh
1.000.000	Millonésimo	Mee-yoh-neh-see-moh
1.500.000	Un millón quinientos milésimo	Oon mee-yohn kee-nee-ehn-tohs mee-leh-see-moh
10.000.000	Diezmillonésimo	Dee_ehs-mee-yoh-neh-see-moh

Decimal Numbers

Talking about decimals in Spanish is fairly simple, there's a formal and an informal nomenclature, and both are widely accepted and understood. However, before you start talking about that, if you're keen on detail, you'll notice that thousands in the previous tables are separated by dots (.) instead of commas (,). This is the way it's done in Spanish; it's opposite to how it's handled in English, so even if it feels weird at first, it won't be hard to learn and remember.

Formal decimal nomenclature starts by naming the whole number as you would read it in cardinal form. The whole number is followed by the word "enteros" (ehn-teh-rohs), which means "wholes". Then the decimals are named the same way, in their cardinal forms, but instead of being followed by "enteros", they're followed by the Spanish word that represents how close they are to the number one in fractions.

If they're a tenth of a one, then they're "décimas" (tenths), followed by "centésimas" (hundredths), and so on. How close they are to one is read easily by just looking at the number of digits after the comma, as you'll see in the following table.

Number of Digits After Comm	Spanish Term	Pronunciation	Translation

a

0,x	Décimas	Deh-see-mahs	Tenths
0,xx	Centésimas	Sehn-teh-see-mahs	Hundredth
0,xxx	Milésimas	Mee-leh-see-mahs	Thousandth
0,xxxx	Diezmilésimas	Dee_ehs-mee-leh-see-mahs	Ten-thousandth
0,xxxxx	Cienmilésimas	See_ehn-mee-leh-see-mahs	Hundred-thousandth
0,xxxxxx	Millonésimas	Mee-yoh-neh-see-mahs	Millionth

Here are a couple of examples of formal decimal nomenclature.

15,76   -   Quince enteros con setenta y seis centésimas.

2,6   -   Dos enteros con seis décimas.

400,234   -   Cuatrocientos enteros con doscientos treinta y cuatro milésimas

Informal decimal nomenclature is far easier, especially because it resembles English decimal nomenclature. Whole numbers are read in their cardinal form, and then they're just followed by "coma" (coh-mah), and then the decimal numbers in their cardinal form. It's also possible to just name the decimals in order as if you were reading a phone number, this is particularly the case when the decimal is too long. Here are some examples of how this could look like.

30,5   -   Treinta coma cinco.

231,46   -   Doscientos treinta y uno coma cuarenta y seis

13,5824169 -   Trece coma cinco ocho veinticuatro dieciséis nueve

Fractions

In Spanish fractions, the numerator is named in its cardinal form, and the denominator is named in its ordinal number if it's between four and ten. If the denominator is a two, it's also correct to call it a half "medio" (meh-deeoh). If the denominator is a three, it can be called "tercio" (tehr-seeoh), which can be translated as third part. Finally, if the denominator is a number higher than ten, then it's named in its cardinal form, but "avos" (ah-bohs) is then added at the end.

3/2   -   Tres medios

24/5   -   Veinticuatro quintos

159/13 treceavos - Ciento cincuenta y nueve

13/4 - Trece cuartos

Articles

Spanish articles are more complicated than English articles. They can also be divided into definite and indefinite articles. Together with adjectives and participle verbs, articles are modified by the gender of the noun they're affecting.

Definite Articles

Definite articles are used when speaking about a known and specific noun. The English definite article is the, while Spanish has four different definite articles.

Definite Article	Pronunciation	Use
El	Ehl	Singular masculine
Los	Lohs	Plural masculine
La	Lah	Singular feminine

| **Las** | Lahs | Plural feminine |

We'll go through a couple of examples to illustrate this.

El perro.

Ehl peh-rroh.

The dog.

Las gaviotas.

Lahs gah-beeoh-tahs.

The seagulls.

Los zapatos.

Lohs sah-pah-tohs.

The shoes.

La computadora.

Lah cohm-poo-tah-doh-rah.

The computer.

It's important to know that in the case of a feminine singular noun that starts with a strong syllable, a masculine article is to be used.

Indefinite Articles

Indefinite articles are used to speak about a non-specific noun. The English indefinite articles are "a" and "an", but in some cases "some" can also be an English equivalent for the Spanish indefinite articles. The Spanish indefinite articles are "un", "unos", "una", and "unas".

Indefinite Article	Pronunciation	Use
Un	Oon	Singular masculine
Unos	Oo-nohs	Plural masculine
Una	Oo-nah	Singular feminine
Unas	Oo-nahs	Plural feminine

Here are some examples that illustrate this.

Una casa.

Oo-nah cah-sah.

A house.

Unos lápices.

Oo-nohs lah-pee-sehs.

Some pencils

Unas gotas.

Oo-nahs goh-tahs.

Some drops.

Un teléfono.

Oon teh-leh-foh-noh.

A phone.

Adjectives

Spanish adjectives have the same role and function as English adjectives. The only difference between Spanish adjectives and English adjectives is that, as previously stated, Spanish adjectives change with the gender of the noun. Here's a list of everyday use adjectives that you must learn, with a couple of examples of how to use them.

Adjective	Pronunciation	Translation
Aburrido	Ah-boo-rree-doh	Boring
Ácido	Ah-see-doh	Acid, sour
Alegre	Ah-leh-reh	Happy, joyful
Alto	Ahl-toh	Tall
Amargo	Ah-mahr-goh	Bitter
Ancho	Ahn-choh	Wide
Azul	Ah-sool	Blue
Bajo	Bah-hoh	Low, short
Blanco	Blahn-coh	White
Blando	Blahn-doh	Soft, bland
Bonito	Boh-nee-toh	Pretty
Bueno	Booeh-noh	Good
Caliente	Cah-lee_ehn-teh	Hot
Capaz	Cah-pahs	Able
Central	Sehn-trahl	Central
Común	Coh-moon	Common

Conocido	Coh-noh-see-doh	Known
Contento	Cohn-tehn-toh	Happy
Corto	Cohr-toh	Short
Débil	Deh-beel	Weak
Delgado	Dehl-gah-doh	Thin
Derecho	Deh-reh-choh	Straight
Diferente	Dee-feh-rehnt	Different
Difícil	Dee-fee-seel	Difficult, hard
Divertido	Dee-behr-tee-doh	Fun
Dulce	Dool-seh	Sweet
Duro	Doo-roh	Hard, tough
Enfermo	Ehn-fehr-moh	Sick
Estrecho	Ehs-treh-choh	Narrow
Fácil	Fah-seel	Easy
Falso	Fahl-soh	Fake
Famoso	Fah-moh-soh	Famous
Feo	Feh-oh	Ugly
Fresco	Frehs-coh	Fresh
Frío	Free-oh	Cold

Fuerte	Fooehr-teh	Strong
Gordo	Gohr-doh	Fat
Grande	Grahn-deh	Big
Guapo	Gooah-poh	Handsome
Húmedo	Oo-meh-doh	Wet
Igual	Ee-gooahl	Equal
Imposible	Eem-poh-see-bleh	Impossible
Interesante	Een-teh-reh-sahn-teh	Interesting
Inútil	Ee-noo-teel	Useless
Joven	Hoh-behn	Young
Largo	Lahr-goh	Long
Lento	Lehn-toh	Slow
Listo	Lees-toh	Smart, clever, ready
Malo	Mah-loh	Bad
Masivo	Mah-see-boh	Massive
Mayor	Mah-yohr	Elder, mayor
Mejor	Meh-hohr	Better
Menor	Meh-nohr	Minor

Natural	Nah-too-rahl	Natural
Negro	Neh-groh	Black
Peor	Peh-ohr	Worse
Pequeño	Peh-kehn-neeoh	Small
Perfecto	Pehr-fec-toh	Perfect
Pobre	Poh-breh	Short
Poco	Poh-coh	Few, scarce, little.
Popular	Poh-poo-lahr	Popular
Posible	Poh-see-bleh	Possible
Rápido	Rah-pee-doh	Fast
Raro	Rah-roh	Rare, weird
Real	Reh-ahl	Real
Recto	Rehc-toh	Straight
Rico	Ree-coh	Rich, yummy, tasteful
Rojo	Roh-hoh	Red
Salado	Sah-lah-doh	Salty
Sano	Sah-noh	Healthy
Seco	Seh-coh	Dry

Simple	Seem-pleh	Simple
Social	Soh-seeahl	Social
Solo	Soh-loh	Lonely, alone
Tímido	Tee-mee-doh	Shy
Tonto	Tohn-toh	Silly, dumb
Triste	Trees-teh	Sad
Útil	Oo-teel	Useful
Verdadero	Behr-dah-deh-roh	True
Verde	Behr-deh	Green
Viejo	Bee_eh-hoh	Old

Adverbs

If adjectives are words that modify the nouns, adverbs are words used to modify the meaning and circumstances surrounding the verbs. Spanish adverbs are divided into six broad categories: time adverbs, place adverbs, modality adverbs, quantity adverbs, affirmation adverbs, and negation adverbs. The first four categories answer the questions "¿Cuándo?" (When?), "¿Dónde?" (Where?), "¿Cómo?" (How?), and "¿Cuánto?" (How much?);

The following two categories are used to make affirmative and negative sentences. Affirmative, negative, and interrogative sentences will be covered in the fifth chapter, we'll focus for now on showing the most common adverbs as well as examples of how they're used. As you'll see in the list, some adverbs appear more than once; that's because some of them fall into more than one category depending on how they're used.

Type of Adverb	Adverb	Pronunciation	Translation
Time Adverb	Ahora	Ah-oh-rah	Now
Time Adverb	Antes	Ahn-tehs	Before
Time Adverb	Después	Dehs-pooehs	After
Time Adverb	Luego	Loo-eh-goh	Later
Time Adverb	Ayer	Ah-yehr	Yesterday
Time Adverb	Hoy	Oh_ee	Today
Time Adverb	Mañana	Mahn-neeah-nah	Tomorrow
Time Adverb	Todavía	Toh-dah-bee-ah	Still

Time Adverb	Aún	Ah_oon	Yet
Time Adverb	Nunca	Noon-cah	Never
Time Adverb	Temprano	Tehm-prah-noh	Early
Time Adverb	Después	Dehs-pooehs	Later
Place Adverb	Ahí	Ah-ee	There
Place Adverb	Aquí	Ah-kee	Here
Place Adverb	Arriba	Ah-rree-bah	Up
Place Adverb	Abajo	Ah-bah-hoh	Down
Place Adverb	Cerca	Sehr-cah	Close, near.
Place Adverb	Detrás	Deh-trahs	Behind
Place Adverb	Fuera	Fooeh-rah	Outside
Place Adverb	Lejos	Leh-hohs	Away

Modality Adverbs	Bien	Bee_ehn	Good
Modality Adverbs	Lentamente	Lehn-tah-mehn-teh	Slowly
Modality Adverbs	Mal	Mahl	Bad
Modality Adverbs	Mejor	Meh-hohr	Better
Modality Adverbs	Peor	Peh-ohr	Worse
Modality Adverbs	Rápidamente	Rah-pee-dah-mehn-teh	Quickly
Quantity Adverbs	Demasiado	Deh-mah-seeah-doh	Too much
Quantity Adverbs	Más	Mahs	Poco
Quantity Adverbs	Menos	Meh-nohs	Less
Quantity Adverbs	Mucho	Moo-choh	A lot, very much, much.
Quantity Adverbs	Nada	Nah-dah	Nothing

Quantity Adverbs	Poco	Poh-coh	Little, small quantity.
Quantity Adverbs	Tanto	Tahn-toh	How much, every one that ____
Quantity Adverbs	Todo	Toh-doh	Everything.
Affirmation Adverbs	Bueno	Booeh-noh	Good
Affirmation Adverbs	Naturalmente	Nah-too-rahl-mehn-teh	Naturally
Affirmation Adverbs	Seguro	Seh-goo-roh	Sure
Affirmation Adverbs	Sí	See	Yes
Affirmation Adverbs	También	Tahm-bee_ehn	Too
Affirmation	Verdaderamente	Behr-dah-deh-rah-	Truly

Adverbs		mehn-teh	
Negation Adverbs	Jamás	Hah-mahs	Never
Negation Adverbs	Nada	Nah-dah	Nothing
Negation Adverbs	No	Noh	No
Negation Adverbs	Ninguno	Neen-goo-noh	None
Negation Adverbs	Nunca	Noon-cah	Never
Negation Adverbs	Tampoco	Tahm-poh-coh	Neither

El caballo corre rápidamente.

Ehl cah-bah-yoh coh-rreh rrah-pee-dah-mehn-teh.

The horse runs quickly.

Jorge trabaja mucho por comprar un coche nuevo.

Hohr-heh trah-bah-hah moo-choh pohr cohm-prahr oon coh-cheh nooeh-boh.

Jorge works hard to buy a new car.

El equipo sigue corriendo aún en la pista.

Ehl eh-kee-poh see-gueh coh-rree_ehn-doh ah_oon ehn lah pees-tah.

The team is still racing on the track.

Adjectives as Adverbs

Some Spanish adjectives can work as adverbs, complementing the verbs depending on the context.

El jugador hace un pase largo hacia el fondo del campo.

Ehl hoo-gah-dohr ah-seh oon pah-seh lahr-goh ah-seeah ehl fohn-doh dehl cahm-poh.

The player makes a long pass to the back of the field.

María cocina delicioso.

Mah-ree-ah coh-see-nah deh-lee-seeoh-soh.

María cooks delicious.

Adverbial Locutions

Adverbial locutions are determined phrases that fulfill the function of an adverb depending on the context.

Type of Adverbial Locution	Adverbial Locution	Pronunciation	Translation
Time Adverbial Locution	A cada paso	Ah cah-dah pah-soh	At each step.
Time Adverbial Locution	A deshora	Ah dehs-oh-rah	Out of time, out of schedule.
Time Adverbial Locution	A diario	Ah deeah-reeoh	Daily
Time Adverbial Locution	Al instante	Ahl eens-tahn-teh	Instantly
Time Adverbial Locution	Al momento	Ahl moh-mehn-toh	At the moment.
Place Adverbial Locution	De cabeza	Deh cah-beh-sah	Upside down.
Place	De aquí	Deh ah-kee	From here

Adverbial Locution	para allá	pah-rah ah-yah	to there.
Modality Adverbial Locution	A ciegas	Ah see_eh-gahs	Blindly
Modality Adverbial Locution	A lo loco	Ah loh loh-coh	Erratically
Modality Adverbial Locution	De improvisto	Deh eem-proh-bees-toh	Suddenly
Modality Adverbial Locution	De raíz	Deh rah-ees	From the root, from the start.
Quantity Adverbial Locution	A tope	Ah toh-peh	To the fullest, to the top.
Affirmation Adverbial Locution	A ciencia cierta	Ah see_ehn-seeah see_ehr-tah	Certainly
Affirmation Adverbial Locution	Con seguridad	Cohn seh-goo-ree-dahd	Surely
Affirmati	Desde	Dehs-deh	Indeed,

on Adverbial Locution	luego	looeh-goh	surely.
Negation Adverbial Locution	De ninguna manera	Deh neen-goo-nah mah-neh-rah	No way at all.
Negation Adverbial Locution	En absoluto	Ehn ab-soh-loo-toh	No way.
Negation Adverbial Locution	Ni en sueños	Nee ehn sooehn-neeohs	Not even in dreams.

No sabemos a ciencia cierta quién rompió la taza.

Noh sah-beh-mohs ah see_ehn-seeah see_ehr-tah kee_ehn rohm-pee_oh lah tah-sah.

We don't know with certainty who broke the cup.

Ella sale a correr a diario.

Eh-yah sah-leh ah coh-rrehr ah deeah-reeoh.

She goes out for a run every day.

Chapter 2: Pronunciation

Spanish pronunciation is generally more straightforward than English pronunciation. English letters and words tend to be pronounced differently depending on where they're placed, but this doesn't happen as often in Spanish. This makes Spanish pronunciation easier to learn from scratch than English pronunciation. With the right approach and a lot of practice, it won't be long before Spanish pronunciation comes naturally to you.

Alphabet

Learning the pronunciation of each individual letter is the fastest and most efficient path to learn Spanish pronunciation.

Vowels

Spanish vowels are always pronounced the same way, no matter where they're placed. These pronunciations are monotonic and simple, so it's easy to learn them. Vowels are also pronounced strongly and with emphasis, so there aren't silent vowels in Spanish, with the exception of "u" under certain specific circumstances.

Also, Spanish vowel pronunciation may be clear, but it's also short. Spanish speakers don't drag vowels the same way as English speakers do unless they want to create emphasis or they have a particular accent. Dragging vowels too much is often the sign of a native English speaker trying to speak Spanish, which is a detail that can be improved with practice.

Consonants

Consonants in Spanish usually have a shorter, softer, and sweeter pronunciation than their equivalents in English. Consonants such as the hard c, k, t, and soft r are notably softer and far more subtle in Spanish than they are in English. In addition, consonants maintain the tendency to always be pronounced the same way, but there are a couple of exceptions, as we'll see in the following segment.

ABC

Letter	Pronunciation
A	Ah, like the A in cat, far more open than your usual English A.
B	Beh, like the b in Bar. With a slightly softer pronunciation.
C	Seh, with a soft and a hard pronunciation.

	The soft pronunciation resembles the C in race, and it happens when the C goes before an I or an E. The hard pronunciation feels more like the C in cat, and it happens when the C goes before an A, O, or U. The hard pronunciation resembles a K, but it's softer and more subtle.
D	Deh, like the D in dice. It's a slightly shorter pronunciation than its English equivalent.
E	Eh, like the E in yell. The E pronunciation goes in the other direction as the A. If the A is very open, the E is a closed pronunciation.
F	Eh-feh, like the F in face.
G	Heh, and as it happens with the C, it has a hard and a soft pronunciation. The hard pronunciation occurs when it goes before an A, O, U, or consonant, and then it's pronounced like the G in great. The soft pronunciation resembles the English H pronunciation, like the H in hoove, and it happens when it precedes I or E.
	Now, here's where the G gets more complicated. If you want a syllable with E or I and a hard G pronunciation, you'll write it with a U and then the U is silent (one of the two only conditions in which the Spanish U is silent). So, GUE is pronounced as GE (hard G), and GUI is pronounced as GI

	(again, hard G pronunciation). If you want to write a syllable with G, U, and I or E, using the hard G pronunciation and where the U isn't silent, then you'll write the U with an umlaut diaeresis, like GÜE or GÜI, as it happens in "pingüino" (penguin), pronounced peen-gooee-noh.
H	Ah-cheh, unlike the English H, the Spanish H is silent, as it happens in the English H pronunciation in honor. The only way that the Spanish H isn't silent is when it's preceded by C.
I	Ee, as the I in big. The Spanish I pronunciation will be represented with EE to convey its sound, but never its duration. The I, just like every other Spanish vowel, must be a shorter pronunciation than its English equivalent.
J	Hoh-tah, and it's pronounced like the English H in happy.
K	Kah, pronounced like the English K in Kathmandu.
L	Eh-leh, pronounced like the English L in lair.
M	Eh-meh, pronounced like the English M in mouse.
N	Eh-neh, pronounced like the English N in

	near.
Ñ	Eh-nee_eh. This letter doesn't exist in the English language, and it's one of the greatest challenges for native English speakers. It's pronounced swiftly and shortly, so the "eh-nee_eh" sound that produces the Spanish ñ is very quick. Think about how you'd pronounce Spanish words with ñ, such as "jalapeño" and you won't have trouble figuring out how to pronounce the Spanish ñ.
O	Oh, pronounced like the English O in bold.
P	Peh, pronounced like the English P in peaceful. This is usually softer than the English P pronunciation.
Q	Coo, pronounced like the English hard C in words such as coat and calm. There's always a U between the Q and the main vowel of the syllable, and this U is silent. This is the second circumstance where the U is silent.
R	Eh-reh, which has a strong pronunciation, a soft pronunciation, and an even stronger pronunciation. The strong pronunciation resembles the English R in race. It's the pronunciation you'd use on an R that stands at the beginning of the work, but it's slightly shorter, and yet still strong. The soft pronunciation is produced like an R that just

barely touches the soft palate of the mouth. It's the R pronunciation you'd use with the R placed anywhere in the middle of the word (in either English or Spanish), and it resembles the pronunciation of the English R in forum, but slightly softer.

The last pronunciation is the rolling R pronunciation that resembles the English R pronunciation in rage. In Spanish, you'll use this pronunciation when you find two Rs put together in a word, and you need to roll an R to achieve it. The rolling R must still be shortish and strong. Drag that rolling R for too long, and it'll be clear you have an accent.

S	Eh-seh, pronounced like the English S in sour. There's no difference between the pronunciation of the Spanish S, Z, and soft C.
T	Teh, pronounced like the English T in torn, but softer.
U	Oo, pronounced like the English Oo in good. Unlike the English U, the Spanish U has a closed and monotone pronunciation.
V	Beh, pronounced like the English B in bad. There's no difference between the pronunciation of the Spanish B and V.
W	Doh-bleh-beh, stands for "double V". The sound used to pronounced W in a word is

	vooeh, the same sound used to pronounce W in English. This is because there are no words born in Spanish with a W, and all Spanish words with a W are no more than English adaptations and are pronounced as such.
X	Eh-kees, pronounced like the English H in have. This would mean that the Spanish pronunciation of X and J are the same.
Y	Yeh, it has a vowel and a consonant pronunciation. The vowel pronunciation is EE, like the Spanish I, and it's pronounced that way when it stands alone, or when it's placed right after a consonant or a vowel preceded by a consonant (as you'd see it in English). As a consonant, it's pronounced like the English Y in yacht and the Spanish LL. It has this pronunciation when it precedes a vowel.
Z	Seh-tah, pronounced like the English Z in zoo. There are no differences between the pronunciation of the Spanish S, Z, and soft C.

Particular Sounds

There are particular sounds and phenomena we should pay attention to that are special in Spanish pronunciation.

Sound	Pronunciation
CH	Traditionally a letter that used to be part of the alphabet, every time the C and H are written together like this, they sound like a harder "SH", like the CH in cheese.
LL	Another sound that used to be part of the traditional Spanish alphabet, two Ls placed together are pronounced as a hard Y, like the English Y in yearn.
Güe	Pronounced as "gooeh".
Güi	Pronounced as "gooee".
Gue	Pronounced like the hard G in "Guess".
Gui	Pronounced like the hard G in "Guild".

Syllable Changes

Sometimes two vowels can be either in the same syllable or two different syllables. This obviously changes the way they're pronounced, written, and also the tilde application rules for the words where these syllables are placed. These special types of syllables are the dipthong, triphthongs, and hiatus, and they're dependent on the concepts of open vowels (a, e, and o) and closed vowels (i, and u).

"Diptongos" or Diphthongs

Diphthongs are syllables with two vowels. This happens when an open vowel (again, a, e, or o) is right next to a closed vowel (i, or u); it's also the case when two closed vowels are placed together. If a dipthong has a tilde, it's always placed in the second vowel. An example of a diphthong is "guapo" (handsome), pronounced gooah-poh with the "u" and the "a" in the same syllable. In this book, dipthongs, which pronunciation can't be written in the same syllable, will be written with an "_" instead of an "-".

"Triptongos" or Triphthongs

As the name implies, tripthongs are syllables with three vowels. They're formed when one open vowel is placed between two closed vowels. If this particular syllable has a tilde, it goes over the open vowel. An example of a triphthong is "buey", pronounced booeh_ee, it's translated as ox. As you can see, "y" in this case work as a vowel as it's pronounced like the Spanish "i".

"Hiato" or Hiatus

The hiatus is the phenomenon when two vowels placed next to each other are part of different syllables. There are many conditions that create a hiatus.

- The two vowels are the same.

- The vowels are two different open vowels.

- The vowels are one open vowel and one closed vowel, but the closed vowel has a tilde. In this case, the rules of tilde placement can be broken because this will always have a tilde. You'll notice there's this kind of hiatus in spoken Spanish when an open vowel and a closed vowel are placed in the same syllable, but the closed vowel is pronounced stronger than the open vowel. In that case, the closed vowel always has a tilde, and it's always a hiatus.

Chapter 3: Nouns & Pronouns

In this chapter we'll cover nouns and mostly pronouns. While Spanish nouns aren't different from English nouns, there are plenty of Spanish pronouns, and it's important to study them thoroughly.

Nouns

As mentioned earlier, Spanish nouns aren't different from English nouns. They're also divided between common nouns and proper nouns, and they're the basis of any language and communication.

"Sustantivos comunes" (soos-tahn-tee-bohs coh-moo-nehs), or common nouns, are those that make reference to any object or person without talking about a specific entity. They're only capitalized at the beginning of sentences (as any other word would), and as mentioned earlier, they're written and pronounced differently depending on the gender.

"Sustantivos propios" (soos-tahn-tee-bohs proh-peeohs), or proper nouns, are nouns that speak about a specific person or entity. These are the ones commonly referred to as names, and they encompass names of persons, animals, geographical locations, books, or anything that's about an individual entity. Proper nouns in Spanish are always written with a capital letter, and with the occasional exception of countries and translated media, they don't need to be translated.

Personal Pronouns

Personal pronouns replace the nouns in those places where the noun is a part or participant entity of the speech. Spanish personal pronouns have a fundamental difference with English personal pronouns in that they have a practical variation when they speak in formal Spanish or informal Spanish.

As you'll see in the following table and examples, the pronoun "usted" and ustedes", used in the second person (but still conjugated in the third person), are formal personal pronouns. Spanish personal pronouns are also often affected by the gender of the noun they're replacing.

Spanish personal pronouns can be divided between subject pronouns and object pronouns. Each one of those two categories has their own subdivisions, and even though not some may be more used than the others, they're all still used very often.

Subject Pronouns

Pronoun	Pronunciation	Translation	Mode
Yo	Yoh	I	First person

			singular
Tú	Too	You	Second person singular (informal)
Usted	Oos-tehd	You	Second person singular (formal)
Él	Ehl	He	Third person singular
Ella	Eh-yah	She	Third person singular
Eso / Esa	Eh-soh	It	Third person singular
Nosotros / Nosotras	Noh-soh-trohs	We	First person plural
Vosotros / Vosotra	Boh-soh-trohs	You	Second person plural (informal

s			)
Ustedes	Oos-teh-dehs	You	Second person plural (formal)
Ellos / Ellas	Eh-yohs	They	Third person plural

As a general rule, Spanish usually skips subject pronouns. The conjugation of the verb is usually enough to know who we are speaking about. However, if for any reason you need to clarify, or if you want to create emphasis, you'll use the subject pronouns. There are a couple of situations where subject pronouns are commonly used in Spanish, and we'll go over them in the examples.

If we want to direct the attention of the person with whom we're conversing about the subject's identity.

¿Puedes ver al chico de la gorra? Él es quien nos llevará a casa.

Pooeh-dehs behr ahl chee-coh deh lah goh-rrah ehl ehs kee_ehn nohs yeh-bah-rah ah cah-sah.

Can you see the guy with the hat? He's the one taking us home.

They're always used to answer questions trying to identify somebody, particularly the subject performing an action.

¿Quién rompió la ventana? Ella lo hizo.

Kee_ehn rohm-peeoh lah behn-tah-nah eh-yah loh ee-soh.

Who broke the window? She did it.

They're used in comparisons between two persons or objects subject to personal pronouns, when the word "que" (translated as "than" in this context) is used.

Tu hermano es más fuerte que yo.

Too ehr-mah-noh ehs mahs fooehr-eh keh yoh.

Your brother is stronger than me.

Object Pronouns

If the subject is the entity that performs the action in the sentence, the object is the objective or goal towards which the action is directed. Object pronouns allow us to convey information regarding individuals and objects in the sentence that aren't the protagonist or subject of the sentence. They're divided between Direct Object Pronouns and Indirect Object Pronouns, which are very similar and often hard to tell from one another.

Direct Object Pronouns

Known in Spanish as "Pronombres de complemento directo" (proh-nohm-brehs deh cohm-pleh-mehn-toh dee-rehc-toh), direct object pronouns replace the nouns that would be the direct target of an action. Direct object pronouns are necessary to understand the verb and the sentence in general.

Pronoun	Pronunciation	Translation	Mode
Me	Meh	Me	First person singular
Te	Teh	You	Second person singular (informal)
Lo	Loh	You	Second person singular (formal)
Lo	Loh	Him, Its	Third person singular

La	Lah	Her	Third person singular
Nos	Nohs	Us	First person plural
Os	Ohs	You	Second person plural (informal)
Les	Lehs	You	Second person plural (formal)
Los / Las	Lohs	Them	Third person plural

Going through some examples of how to use direct object pronouns correctly, they're written without prepositions, and they usually speak about objects.

¿Haz visto mis zapatos? No los encuentro.

Ahs bees-toh mees sah-pah-tohs noh lohs ehn-cooehn-troh.

Have you seen my shoes? I can't find them.

Sentences with the verbs "querer" (to love or to want), "esperar" (to wait), "invitar" (to invite), "llamar" (to call), among others that speak of actions always directed to a person or living being always use direct object pronouns referring to persons.

¿Sabes algo de Juan? Lo llamo y no me atiende.

Sah-behs ahl-goh deh hooahn loh yah-moh ee noh meh ah-tee_ehn-deh.

Do you know anything about Juan? I keep calling him, but he doesn't answer me.

Indirect Object Pronoun

Difficult to tell apart from direct object pronouns, indirect object pronouns convey information about the goal of the action in the sentence, which is always a living being (person or animal).

It's often the case that when the direct object pronoun tells you about the object that receives the action, the indirect object pronoun will tell you for whom the action is intended. For example, if you were to speak about cooking a meal for your family, the direct object of the sentence would be the meal, and the indirect object of the sentence would be, in this case, your family.

Indirect object pronouns are the same as direct object pronouns in the first and second person, but they change in the third person.

Pronoun	Pronunciation	Translation	Mode
Me	Meh	Me	First person singular
Te	Teh	You	Second person singular (informal)
Le	Leh	You	Second person singular (formal)
Le	Leh	Him, her, its	Third person singular
Se	Seh	Him, her, Its	Third person singular
Nos	Nohs	Us	First person plural

Os	Ohs	You	Second person plural (informal)
Les	Lehs	You	Second person plural (informal)
Les	Lehs	They	Third person plural
Se	Seh	They	Third person plural

If you're wondering why there seems to be two pronouns in third person that mean the same in both singular and plural, that's because "se", the second one, isn't always used. It's used as a replacement for the pronoun "le" or "les" when there's also a direct object pronoun "lo", "la", "los", or "las" in the sentence. This way, oddly sounding and confusing sentences are avoided. We'll illustrate this with an example.

Espero que mis hijos traten bien el carro, ya se los he prestado antes.

Ehs-peh-roh keh mees ee-hos trah-tehn bee_ehn ehl cah-rroh yah seh lohs eh prehs-tah-doh ahn-tehs.

I hope my children treat the car well. I've already lent it to them before.

There are two facts that are important regarding direct and indirect object pronoun placement. First, both direct and indirect object pronouns are always placed before the verb. And second, if indirect and direct object pronouns are used in the same sentence, the indirect object pronoun is always used first.

Prepositional Pronouns

"Pronombres preposicionales" (proh-nohm-brehs preh-poh-see-seeoh-nah-lehs) or prepositional pronouns are used right after prepositions. This means that they have a similar function to object pronouns, but in this case, prepositional pronouns aren't necessarily the object of a verb or action. We'll start with a list of the most common prepositions in Spanish so that we can go over to prepositional pronouns from there.

Preposition	Pronunciation	Translation
A	Ah	At / To
Antes de	Ahn-tehs deh	Before

De	Deh	From (as in fom-to).
Dentro de	Dehn-troh deh	Inside
Desde	Dehs-deh	From / Since
Después de	Dehs-pooehs de	After
Durante	Doo-rahn-teh	During
En	Ehn	In (for months, seasons, years, and particular dates).
Hasta	Ahs-tah	Until
Por	Pohr	In (time of the day).
Sobre	Soh-breh	Over
Tras	Trahs	After (when talking about something that happens after something else).

We'll cover the prepositional pronouns, and then we'll show a pair of examples of how they're used.

Pronoun	Pronunciation	Translation	Mode
Mí	Mee	Me	First person singular
Ti	Tee	You	Second person singular (informal)
Usted	Oohs-tehd	You	Second person singular (formal)
Él	Ehl	He	Third person singular
Ella	Eh-yah	She	Third person singular
Ello	Eh-yoh	It	Third person singular
Sí	See	Himself, herself, Itself	Third person singular
Nosotros / Nosotras	Noh-soh-trohs	We	First person plural

Vosotros / Vosotras	Boh-soh-trohs	You	Second person plural (informal)
Ustedes	Oos-teh-dehs	You	Second person plural (formal)
Ellos / Ellas	Eh-yohs	They	Third person plural
Sí	See	Themselves	Third person plural

Mi hermano se compró una pizza para sí solo.

Mee ehr-mah-noh seh cohm-proh oo-nah pee-sah pah-rah see soh-loh.

My brother bought a pizza for himself.

Tu novio no quiere ver la película sin ti.

Too noh-beeoh noh kee_eh-reh behr lah peh-lee-coo-lah seen tee.

Your boyfriend doesn't want to see the movie without you.

There are two important exceptions to the rule of preposition pronouns, and it's in first and second person singular with the prepositions "entre" (between) and "según" (according to). In these cases, it's incorrect to use the pronouns "mí" and "ti", and instead, the subject pronouns "yo" and "tú" should be used.

Según tú, no deberíamos comprar esta computadora.

Se-goon too noh deb-beh-ree-ah-mohs cohm-prahr ehs-tah cohm-poo-tah-doh-rah.

According to you, we shouldn't buy this computer.

Esta competencia es entre tú y yo.

Ehs-tah cohm-peh-tehn-seeah ehs ehn-treh too ee yoh.

This competition is between you and me.

Possessive Pronouns

Possessive pronouns are used to convey possession and relationship ties. As a pronoun, it's affected by the gender and number of the replaced nouns. There are possessive pronouns when they behave as such, replacing the noun, and possessive determinants when they appear next to the noun.

Possessive Pronouns

"Pronombres posesivos" (Proh-nohm-brehs poh-seh-see-bohs) or possessive pronouns are the ones that replace the noun. These are affected by the gender and noun they're replacing, and they're always preceded by a definite article.

Pronoun	Pronunciation	Translation	Mode
Mío / Mía	Mee-oh	Mine	First person singular
Tuyo / Tuya	Too-yoh	Yours	Second person singular (informal)
Suyo / Suya	Soo-yoh	Yours	Second person singular (formal)
Suyo / Suya	Soo-yoh	His, hers, its.	Third person singular
Nuestro / Nuestra	Nooehs-troh	Ours	First person plural

Vuestro / Vuestra	Booehs-troh	Yours	Second person plural (informal)
Suyo / Suya	Soo-yoh	Yours	Second person plural (formal)
Suyo / Suya	Soo-yoh	Theirs	Third person plural

Mi teléfono está sobre la mesa, y el tuyo está en el cuarto.

Mee teh-leh-phoh-noh ehs-tah soh-breh lah meh-sah ee ehl too-yoh ehs-tah ehn ehl cooahr-toh.

My phone is on the table, and yours is in the bedroom.

Ese perro que estás acariciando se parece al de Gabriela. Creo que no es el mío si no el suyo.

Eh-seh peh-rroh keh ehs-tahs ah-cah-ree-seeahn-doh seh pah-reh-seh ahl deh gah-bree_eh-lah creh-oh keh noh ehs ehl mee_oh see noh ehl soo-yoh.

That dog you're petting looks like Gabriela's. I believe it's not mine but hers.

Possessive Determinants

Possessive determinants are words that convey ownership or filiation over or with something, but they appear next to the noun instead of replacing it (like a pronoun). The gender and the number of possessive determinants always matches one of the possessed objects. There are two groups of possessive determinants, there are tonic possessive determinants and atonic possessive determinants.

Atonic Possessive Determinants

"Determinantes posesivos átonos" (deh-tehr-mee-nahn-tehs poh-seh-see-bohs ah-toh-nohs) or atonic possessive determinants are placed right before the noun of the possessed or filiated object or person. As you'll see in the following table, only the first and second plural person have a feminine alteration to the determinant.

Pronoun	Pronunciation	Translation	Mode
Mi	Mee	My	First person singular
Tu	Too	Your	Second person singular

			(informal)
Su	Soo	Your	Second person singular (formal)
Su	Soo	His, her, its.	Third person singular
Nuestro / Nuestra	Nooehs-troh	Our	First person plural
Vuestro / Vuestra	Booehs-troh	Your	Second person plural (informal)
Suyo / Suya	Soo-yoh	Yours	Second person plural (formal)
Suyo / Suya	Soo-yoh	Theirs	Third person plural

Mi coche está limpio.

Mee coh-cheh ehs-tah leem-peeoh.

My car is clean.

Tu asiento es este, junto al mío.

Too ah-see_ehn-toh ehs ehs-teh hoon-toh ahl mee-oh.

Your seat is this one, next to mine.

If you're confused by the second person singular informal equivalent of the atonic possessive determinants "tu" and its resemblance to the second person singular subject pronoun, pay attention to the tilde. The later "tú" always has a tilde, while the first one "tu" is never written with a tilde.

Tonic Possessive Determinants

"Determinantes posesivos tónicos" (deh-tehr-mee-nahn-tehs poh-seh-see-bohs toh-nee-cohs) or tonic possessive determinants are always placed right after the noun of the object they possess or filiate to. They're written and pronounced exactly the same way as possessive pronouns, but in this case, they're written next to the possessed noun instead of replacing it.

Pronoun	Pronunciation	Translation	Mode

Mío / Mía	Mee-oh	Of mine	First person singular
Tuyo / Tuya	Too-yoh	Of yours	Second person singular (informal)
Suyo / Suya	Soo-yoh	Of yours	Second person singular (formal)
Suyo / Suya	Soo-yoh	His, her, its.	Third person singular
Nuestro / Nuestra	Nooehs-troh	Of ours	First person plural
Vuestro / Vuestra	Booehs-troh	Of yours	Second person plural (informal)
Suyo / Suya	Soo-yoh	Of yours	Second person plural (formal)
Suyo / Suya	Soo-yoh	Of theirs	Third person plural

El dueño de este bar es un buen amigo mío.

Ehl dooehn-neeoh deh ehs-teh bahr ehs oon booehn ah-mee-goh mee-oh.

The owner of this bar is a good friend of mine.

¡Ven a ver lo que está haciendo la hija tuya!

Behn ah behr loh keh ehs-tah ah-see_ehn-doh lah ee-hah too-yah

Come see what your daughter is doing!

Reflexive Pronouns

Reflexive pronouns are always used with a reflexive verb and vice versa. If we were to define reflexive verbs, we'd say they're always accompanied by a reflexive pronoun, and they're used to describe an action the subject of the sentence is performing over himself or herself. This is the main and only function of the reflexive pronouns, so it's not hard to know when they're used.

Pronoun	Pronunciation	Translation	Mode

Me	Meh	Myself	First person singular
Te	Teh	Yourself	Second person singular (informal)
Se	Seh	Yourself	Second person singular (formal)
Se	Seh	His, her, its	Third person singular
Nosotros / Nosotras	Noh-soh-trohs	Ourselves	First person plural
Vosotros / Vosotras	Boh-soh-trohs	Yourselves	Second person plural (informal)
Ustedes	Oos-teh-dehs	Yourselves	Second person plural (formal)
Ellos / Ellas	Eh-yohs	Theirs	Third person plural

Regarding the plural variants of the reflexive pronouns, the fact that they're the same as the subject pronouns can be confusing. Discerning between the two of them is a matter of context. If the sentence spins around a reflexive verb, hence, a verb that the subject is performing over himself, then it's a reflexive pronoun even though in those three cases it's written the same way as the subject pronouns.

Depending on the conjugation of the reflexive verb, the reflexive pronoun can either go before the verb as a separate word, or right after the verb, attached to it, in two particular cases. Since there are more occasions in which it's correct to place it before the verb, we'll point out when to place it after the verb.

It's placed right after the verb, attached to it, in positive imperative verb conjugations.

¡Vístete antes de salir!

Bees-teh-teh ahn-tehs deh sah-leer

Get dressed before going out!

However, in negative imperative verb conjugations, it's placed before the reflexive verb as a separate word.

¡No te comas la pasta sin cubiertos!

Noh teh coh-mahs lah pahs-tah seen coo-bee_ehr-tohs

Don't eat the pasta without cutlery.

It can go after the verb in its infinitive conjugation.

Ella va a bañarse.

Eh-yah bah ah bahn-neeahr-seh.

She's going to bathe herself.

In the conjugation of the verb to be + gerund, the reflexive pronoun can either go before or after the reflexive verb.

Él se está comiendo la pasta.

Ehl seh ehs-tah coh-mee_ehn-doh lah pahs-tah.

He's eating the pasta.

Él se la está comiendo.

Ehl seh lah ehs-tah coh-mee_ehn-doh.

He's eating it.

Interrogative Pronouns

Interrogative pronouns, next to the interrogative adverbs, are part of the interrogative words. Since interrogative pronouns are the same as interrogative adverbs and even relative pronouns, it can get complicated to tell them apart. We'll be able to tell them from one another when we look at the function that they fulfill.

In the case of interrogative pronouns, their function is to ask for the noun in a question. As pronouns, they always replace the noun, but interrogative pronouns, as well as all interrogative words, are used to ask for information instead of giving or communicating information. With interrogative pronouns, the information they ask for is a noun, an individual entity.

Interrogative Pronoun	Pronunciation	Translation
Qué	Keh	What
Quién	Kee_ehn	Who
Cuál	Cooahl	Which

Technically these three are the only interrogative pronouns. The remaining interrogative words fall into the category of interrogative adverbs or relative pronouns. The use of the three interrogative pronouns can be confusing for non-native Spanish speakers, so this is where we'll focus on when we go through the examples.

Use of "Quién"

"Quién" isn't interchangeable with the other interrogative pronouns. It has only one use, and it is to ask for the identity of a person or group of persons. It's adapted to the number of persons that it's asking about.

¿Quién se comió mi almuerzo?

Kee_ehn seh coh-meeoh mee ahl-mooehr-soh

Who ate my lunch?

¿Quiénes vienen con nosotros a la playa?

Kee_eh-nehs bee_eh-nehn cohn noh-soh-trohs ah lah plah-yah

Who's coming with us to the beach?

Use of "Qué" and "Cuál"

"Qué" and "cuál" are particularly difficult to tell apart when you want to use either one or the other. "Qué" is used to identify something, while "cuál" points out something. We'll see a couple of examples of how these distinctions work, which is important because if you want to be a technical Spanish speaker, you shouldn't use one of these terms in place of the other one.

You'll want to use "Qué" + "Verb" whenever you want to identify an element of any category.

¿Qué lees? – Leo el periódico.

Keh leh-ehs leh-oh ehl peh-reeoh-dee-coh.

What are you reading? – I'm reading the newspaper.

¿Qué comes? – Una hamburguesa.

Keh coh-mehs oo-nah ahm-boor-guess-sah.

What are you eating? – A hamburger.

If you want to ask about a category or groups without giving options, you'd still use "qué". This is when the available options aren't limited, but instead, every single element that's part of that category are part of it. In these cases, when you want to ask about an element that's not immediately present, you'll need to use a noun, in which case you'll use "qué" + "noun" + "verb".

¿Qué género de literatura te gusta más?

Keh heh-neh-roh deh lee-teh-rah-too-rah teh –goos-tah mahs

What genre of literature do you like the most?

¿Qué país te ha gustado más?

Keh pah-ees teh ah goos-tah-doh mahs

Which country did you like the most?

You can also use "cuál" to make an open question with unlimited possible answers in any given category, as in the previous example. However, in this case, the verb needs to come first.

¿Cuál es tu banda favorita?

Cooahl ehs too bahn-dah fah-boh-ree-tah

Which one is your favorite band?

¿Cuál compraste ayer?

Cooahl cohm-prahs-teh ah-yehr

Which one did you buy yesterday?

Besides making open questions, "cuál" also allows us to make a question with limited answers. In this case, you'll use "cuál" + "verb" + "selection of elements or possible answers".

¿Cuál debería ponerme hoy, el rojo o el negro?

Cooahl deh-beh-ree-ah poh-nehr-meh oh_ee ehl roh-hoh oh ehl neh-groh

Which one shall I wear today, red or black?

¿Cuál película quieres ver, esta o esta?

Cooahl peh-lee-coo-lah kee_eh-rehs behr ehs-tah oh ehs-tah

Which movie do you want to see, this one or this one?

Relative Pronouns

Relative pronouns are pronouns used to give way to relative sentences; the last ones are sentences secondary or dependent to a main sentence. Relative sentences give information that complements what's being said in the main sentence. Some of the relative pronouns are written the same way as the interrogative pronouns.

However, unlike interrogative pronouns, relative pronouns don't have a tilde. Unlike most other pronouns, relative pronouns remain the same no matter the grammatical person; the only variation they have is that some of them change with the gender and the number of the noun they're replacing or referencing.

Relative Pronoun	Pronunciation	Translation
Que	Keh	That
El que / La que / Los que / Las que	Ehl keh	At which, the one which, to which
El cual / La cual / Los cuales / Las cuales	Ehl cooahl	Which
Quien / Quienes	Kee_eh-nehs	Who, at whom
Cuyo / Cuya / Cuyos / Cuyas	Coo-yoh	Whose
Cuanto / Cuanta / Cuantos / Cuantas	Cooahn-toh	How many, those who

Relative sentences can either be at the middle of the sentence between commas, or at the end of the sentence. If they're trying to explain something, adding knowledge and context to the main sentence, then they should be placed at the middle of the main sentence between commas, like this:

Mi amigo, quien compró la pizza de ayer, vino hoy a jugar videojuegos.

Mee ah-mee-goh kee_ehn cohm-proh lah pee-sah deh ah-yehr bee-noh oh_ee ah hoo-gahr bee-dee-oh-hooeh-gohs.

My friend, who bought the pizza yesterday, came today to play video games.

If instead, the relative sentence is trying to specify something, then it should be placed at the end of the main sentence. Instead of adding context to the main sentence, they narrow down its meaning to specifics, like this:

Quiero que compres el vestido, el que vimos ayer en la tienda.

Kee_eh-roh keh cohm-prehs ehl behs-tee-doh ehl keh bee-mohs ah-yehr ehn lah tee_ehn-dah.

I want you to buy the dress, the one we saw yesterday at the store.

We'll go over the different relative pronouns with examples of how they're used.

Use of "Que"

"Que" is the most common relative pronoun in Spanish since it allows us to talk about anything. It can be used with explicative and specifier sentences with no limitation except for never being preceded by a preposition. In order to place a preposition before the relative pronoun "que", it's necessary to place a definite article between them, and that's considered the next relative pronoun.

Él está usando un sombrero que es de su padre.

Ehl ehs-tah oo-sahn-doh oon sohm-breh-roh keh ehs deh soo pah-dreh.

He's wearing a hat that is his father's.

Use of "El que"

"El que" as a relative pronoun can be used to speak about either a person or an object. When it's not preceded by a preposition, then it can only be used in explicative relative sentences, like this:

El doctor de ayer, el que te curó, vino hoy otra vez.

Ehl dohc-tohr deh ah-yehr ehl keh teh coo-roh bee-noh oh_ee oh-trah behs.

Yesterday's doctor, the one that healed you, came back today.

And if it's preceded by a preposition, then it can be used in either explicative and specifier sentences, like this:

Quiero que me compres un helado, el que compraste ayer estaría bien.

Kee_eh-oh keh meh cohm-prehs oon eh-lah-doh ehl keh cohm-prahs-teh ah-yehr ehs-tah-ee-ah bee_ehn.

I want you to buy me ice cream, the one you bought yesterday would be fine.

We won't go over the use of "el cual" as it's equivalent to "el que". Both of these are used the same way, and therefore the only reason to use one instead of the other is to provide variation to the text. Also, "el cual" is often considered more formal than "el que".

Use of "Lo que"

"Lo que" is used to replace a whole sentence instead of just a noun. When it's used, it replaces a whole phrase.

Ella está muy feliz hoy, a pesar de lo que pasó ayer.

Eh-yah ehs-tah mooee feh-lees oh_ee ah peh-sahr deh loh keh pah-soh ah-yehr.

She's very happy today, in spite of what happened yesterday.

As you saw in the previous example, "lo que" is replacing the whole context of what happened the day prior. "Lo cual" isn't going to be covered as it has the same use as "lo que". Either one of them can be used instead of the other.

Use of "Quien"

The relative pronoun "quien" can only be used to speak about a person. It's so formal that it's usually only seen in written Spanish. If it's not preceded by a preposition, then it's similar to "que" in explicative relative sentences, like this:

Mi perro, quien todos los días se porta bien, esperó a que viniera mi abuela para romper su bolso.

Mee peh-rroh kee_ehn toh-dohs lohs dee-ahs seh pohr-ah bee_ehn ehs-peh-roh ah keh bee-nee_eh-rah mee ah-booeh-lah pah-rah rohm-pehr soo bohl-soh.

My dog, who behaves correctly every single day, waited for my grandmother to come to break her bag.

If "quien" is instead preceded by a preposition, then it has a similar use to "el que", and can be used in sentences both explicative and specifier relative sentences.

Vamos a ver a mi primo hoy, con quien pasaremos la noche en el bar.

Bah-mohs ah behr ah mee pree-moh oh_ee cohn kee_ehn pah-sah-reh-mohs lah noh-cheh ehn ehl bahr.

We're going to see my cousin today, with whom we'll spend the night at the bar.

Use of "Cuyo"

The relative pronoun "cuyo" replaces the person that owns or is related to an object or person right beside the relative pronoun. Relative pronoun changes in gender and number with the owned object or filiated person, not with the subject it's replacing. It can be used in either explicative or specifier relative sentences, and it's usually limited to formal language and written texts.

Gabriel, cuya moto se averió esta mañana, llegó tarde hoy.

Gah-bee_ehl coo-yah moh-toh seh ah-beh-reeoh ehs-tah mahn-neeah-nah yeh-goh tahr-deh oh_ee.

Gabriel, whose motorcycle broke down this morning, arrived late today.

Use of "Cuanto"

The relative pronoun "cuanto" replaces a certain number of persons, animals, or objects. It's written instead of "all of the...", expressing that the totality of items that are members of that group. It can be used for either explicative or specifier relative sentences.

La alarma sonó alertando a todos, cuantos estaban preparados corrieron a alistarse.

Lah ah-alhr-mah soh-noh ah-lehr-tahn-doh ah toh-dohs cooahn-tohs ehs-tah-bahn preh-pah-rah-dohs coh-rree_eh-rohn ah ah-lees-tahr-seh.

The alarm rang alerting everyone. All of those who were ready ran to prepare themselves.

Demostrative Pronouns

Demonstrative pronouns (and determinants) are used to point out a person, object, or animal, while also conveying information regarding its distance away from the speaker. There are three Spanish adverbs that speak about distance.

There's "aquí" (ah-kee), which can be translated as "here". There's "ahí" (ah-ee), which can be translated as "there", speaking about objects that are relatively close. Finally, there's "allí" (ah-yee), which can also be translated as "there" but for objects that are further away. These three conceptualized distances depend on the context and the comparison of the relative distances of the different objects in the conversation. The three demonstrative pronouns use these three concepts when describing the object and its relationship with the speaker.

There are demonstrative pronouns and demonstrative determinants, and they're written exactly the same way, with the exception that demonstrative determinants don't have a neutral form.

Demonstrative Pronoun	Pronunciation	Translation
Este / Esta / Estos / Estas/ Eso	Ehs-teh	This one, these ones
Ese / Esa / Esos / Esas / Eso	Eh-seh	That one, those ones
Aquel / Aquella / Aquellos / Aquellas / Aquello	Ah-kehl	That one, those ones

Here's an additional table that will illustrate how and when exactly these demonstrative pronouns are used.

Grammatical Person	Demonstrative Pronoun "Aquí"	Demonstrative Pronoun "Ahí"	Demonstrative Pronoun "Allí"
Masculine singular	Este	Ese	Aquel
Masculine plural	Estos	Esos	Aquellos
Feminine singular	Esta	Esa	Aquella
Feminine plural	Estas	Esas	Aquellas
Neutral form	Esto	Eso	Aquello

Demonstrative Pronouns Use

As they're the same, you'll know that these are demonstrative pronouns when there's no noun next to it. As long as it's replacing a noun in the sentence, then it's a pronoun.

¿Puedo probarme esta camisa?

Pooeh-doh proh-bahr-meh ehs-tah cah-mee-sah

Can I try on this shirt?

You'll also know that it's a demonstrative pronoun whenever you use a neutral demonstrative. Neutral demonstrative are only used in singular form, and they speak about something that's unknown or something that the speaker is unwilling to name.

No sé qué significa eso.

Noh seh keh seeg-nee-fee-cah eh-soh.

I don't know what that means.

Demonstrative Determinants

Demonstrative determinants are the same as demonstrative pronouns, except that demonstrative determinants don't have neutral form. They're always placed before a noun, and they match in gender and name with this noun.

¿Me pasas ese bolso por favor?

Meh pah-sahs eh-seh bohl-soh pohr fah-bohr

Can you hand me that bag please?

Demonstrative pronouns and determinants can be used to communicate geographical distances, but also time differences. "Aquí" can be used to speak about the present, "ahí" about the recent past, and "allí" about the past that's further away.

¿Recuerdas lo bien que la pasamos aquel verano en la playa?

Reh-cooehr-dahs loh bee_ehn keh lah pah-sah-mohs ah-kehl beh-rah-noh ehn lah plah-yah

Do you remember how much fun we had that summer on the beach?

Indefinite Pronouns

Indefinite pronouns and determinants are used to express the identity or quantity of something without being specific. They're used to talk vaguely, so their equivalents in the English language are something, some, several, someone, nobody, another one, anyone, a couple, a few, etc. Some indefinite terms can only be used as indefinite determinants as they must always precede a noun, while others can be used as indefinite pronouns.

Indefinite Term	Pronunciation	Translation	Variability
Algún / Alguno / Alguna /	Ahl-goon	Some	Gender and

Algunos / Algunas			number.
Otro / Otra / Otros / Otras	Oh-troh	Another	Gender and number.
Mucho / Mucha / Muchos / Muchas	Moo-choh	Many, a lot, too much.	Gender and number.
Poco / Poca / Pocos / Pocas	Poh-coh	A few, a couple.	Gender and number.
Demasiado / Demasiada / Demasiados / Demasiadas	Deh-mah-seeah-doh	Too much, too many.	Gender and number.
Todo / Toda / Todos / Todas	Toh-doh	Everyone, everything, every, all.	Gender and number.
Tanto / Tanta /	Than-toh	So much,	Gender and

Tantos / Tantas		so many.	number.
Cierto / Cierta / Cierttos / Ciertas	See_ehr-toh	Certain.	Gender and number.
Bastante / Bastantes	Bahs-than-the	Many, plenty of.	Only number.
Quienquiera / Qienesquiera	Kee_ehn-kee_eh-rah	Whomever, whomsoever.	Only number.
Cualquier / Cualesquiera	Cooahl-kee_ehr	Any, anyone.	Only number.
Varios / Varias	Bah-reeohs	Several	Only gender.
Ningún / Ninguno / Ninguna	Neen-goon	None, any, none of.	Only gender.
Alguien	Ahl-guee_ehn	Someone	Doesn't change.
Algo	Ahl-goh	Something	Doesn't change.

Más	Mahs	More, -er.	Doesn't change.
Menos	Meh-nohs	Less	Doesn't change.
Nada	Nah-dah	Nothing	Doesn't change.
Nadie	Nah-dee_eh	Nobody, no one.	Doesn't change.
Cada	Cah-dah	Each, each one, every.	Doesn't change.
Cualquiera	Cooahl-kee_eh-rah	Anyone, any.	Doesn't change.

Indefinite Pronouns

These don't have the noun next to them, but they still match in gender and number with it.

Todos dijeron que cantaste muy bien.

Toh-dohs dee-heh-rohn keh cahn-tahs-teh mooee bee_ehn.

They all said you sang very well.

Indefinite Determinant

Much more common in the Spanish language, indefinite determinants are placed next to a noun, with which they match in gender and number if possible.

Ella toca varios instrumentos.

Eh-yah toh-cah bah-reeohs eens-troo-mehn-tohs.

She plays several instruments.

Double Negation

In Spanish, the double negation created by combining indefinite pronouns such as "nadie" (nobody) and no is not only advised but necessary. Negative sentences with one of these indefinite pronouns also need the negation of the verb.

Ella no se comió nada de su desayuno.

Eh-yah noh seh coh-meeoh nah-dah deh soo deh-sah-yoo-noh.

She didn't eat any of her breakfast.

Chapter 4: Verbs

Spanish verbs are considered one of the hardest points to learn for non-native Spanish speakers. Considered complicated even by native Spanish speakers, verb conjugation in Spanish can be tricky. However, if you learn verb conjugation in order, going from regular verb conjugation to irregular verb conjugation, and you pay attention to the patterns, you'll learn this in no time. Once you understand the basics, the experience will polish the edges of verb conjugations.

Impersonal Verb Conjugations

There are three very basic verb conjugations that must be understood before learning about regular verb conjugation; the infinitive, participle, and gerund conjugations. These are the forms used by verbs when they're used in impersonal voices, which is why they're considered to be basic forms of the verbs.

Infinitive Verb Conjugation

Out of the three impersonal verb conjugations, the infinitive conjugation is considered to be the baseline form of all Spanish verbs. The English equivalent of infinitive is To + The Verb, but that's not how it works in Spanish. The Spanish infinitive is formed with the base verb + one of the three verbal suffixes "ar", "er", or "ir". This means that by looking at the infinitive conjugation of a verb you'll know the base of that verb, and also which one of the three verbal suffixes does it have. This information is vital for regular verb conjugation, as we'll see in the following segment of this chapter.

Pienso cocinar pescado hoy.

Pee_ehn-soh coh-see-nahr pehs-cah-doh oh_ee.

I plan to cook fish today.

Infinitive conjugation isn't affected by gender or number, and as it happens in English, Spanish infinitive verb conjugations can also be used as a noun, like this:

Tocar guitarra es mi pasión.

Toh-cahr guee-tah-rrah ehs mee pah-seeohn.

Playing guitar is my passion.

Participle Verb Conjugation

Spanish participle verbs are conjugated by taking the base form of the verb and adding one of two suffixes. The suffix "ado" (ah-doh) is added when the infinitive suffix of the verb is "ar". If the infinitive suffix of the verb is "er" or "ir", then the participle verb suffix is "ido".

Participle verbs are used in the construction of verb tenses. However, unlike English participle verbs that are used for progressive tenses, Spanish participle verb conjugations is used in some past and future verb conjugations (more on this in the sixth chapter).

Ella ha viajado todo el año.

Eh-yah ah beeah-hah-doh toh-doh ehl ahn-neeoh.

She has traveled all year.

Besides verbs, participle verbs can sometimes be used as conjunctions, like the verb "deber" (deh-behr), which is conjugated in its participle form in the following example as "debido" (due to) and works as a participle verb.

Ellos fueron al hospital debido a que su abuelo se enfermó.

Eh-yohs fooeh-rohn ahl ohs-pee-tahl deh-bee-doh ah keh soo ah-booeh-loh seh ehn-fehr-moh.

They went to the hospital because their grandfather got sick.

Spanish participle verbs can also work as adjectives. If participle verbs work as adjectives, then in those cases they're also affected by gender like any other adjective, as mentioned in the first chapter. We'll illustrate this with the participle conjugation of "mojar" (to wet) as an adjective.

Mi ropa mojada me da frío.

Mee roh-pah moh-hah-dah meh dah free-oh.

My wet clothes make me cold.

Irregular Participle Conjugations

There are two situations in which the conjugation of the participle verb isn't exactly the same as previously described.

The first situation is easy to remember, and it's when the base of the verb ends with a vowel and it's conjugated with the participle suffix "ido". In this case, you must make an hiatus placing a tilde in the i of "ido". Take for example "leer" (le-ehr), translated as to read, its participle conjugation is leído, with a tilde in the i to form the hiatus.

The second situation doesn't follow a pattern and you'll need to memorize it. In this case, the verbs have a participle conjugation that strays far away from the normal participle conjugation pattern. Here is a list of the most common verbs that have an irregular participle conjugation with an asterisk on those verbs that can also be conjugated normally in the participle conjugation. However, even though these couple of verbs can be conjugated normally, their irregular conjugations are the ones used the most.

Verb	Pronunciation	Irregular Participle Conjugation	Pronunciation	Translation
Abrir	Ah-breer	Abierto	Ah-bee_ehr-toh	To open
Decir	Deh-seer	Dicho	Dee-choh	To say
Escribir	Ehs-cree-beer	Escrito	Ehs-cree-toh	To write
Freír *	Freh-eer	Frito	Free-toh	To fry
Imprimir *	Eem-pree-meer	Impreso	Eem-preh-soh	To print
Morir	Moh-reer	Muerto	Mooehr-toh	To die
Poner	Poh-nehr	Puesto	Pooehs-toh	To place, to put somewhere

Proveer *	Proh-beh-her	Provisto	Proh-bees-toh	To provide
Suscribir	Soos-cree-beer	Suscrito	Soos-cree-toh	To subscribe
Ver	Behr	Visto	Bees-toh	To see
Volver	Bohl-behr	Vuelto	Booehl-toh	To return

Gerund Verb Conjugation

The Spanish gerund verb conjugation takes the function of the English verb conjugation by creating progressive tenses. Spanish gerund, unlike English gerund, works as a verb. Also, Spanish gerund isn't affected by gender, number, or grammatical person, as it happens with the infinitive.

Spanish gerund is constructed with the base form of the verb and adding the suffixes "ando" or "iendo". If the infinitive suffix of the verb is "ar" you'll add "ando", and if it's "er" or "ir" you'll add "iendo" as gerund suffix. The main function of the Spanish gerund verb conjugation is to speak about something going on at the moment, which means that the gerund is used to speak in progressive tenses.

Estamos viajando juntos hacia Japón.

Ehs-tah-mohs beeah-han-doh hoon-tohs ah-seeah hah-pohn.

We're traveling to Japan together.

Irregular Gerund Conjugation

As it happens with the participle conjugation, some verbs aren't conjugated following the strict pattern for Spanish gerund verb conjugation.

1. The most common exception to the regular gerund conjugation pattern is when the base of the verb ends with a vowel, and its gerund suffix is "iendo". In this case, the verb will be conjugated with "yendo" instead of "iendo" to form the gerund. We'll take, for example, "leer" once again, which is conjugated as "leyendo" in Spanish gerund.

2. If the base of the verb ends with an ll or an ñ, and its gerund suffix is "iendo", then the i of "iendo" is omitted in the Spanish gerund conjugation. We'll take, for example, the verb "gruñir" (to growl). The gerund conjugation of that verb is "gruñendo" instead of "gruñiendo".

3. For verbs that have an "e" in their base form and end with "ir" as infinitive suffix, change this "e" to an "i" in the Spanish gerund conjugation. If we look at "mentir" (to lie), its

right gerund conjugation would be "mintiendo", not "mentiendo".

4. The last irregular conjugation pattern for the Spanish gerund is when the verb has an o in its base form and either "er" or "ir" as infinitive suffix. If these conditions are met and also the verb's "o" is changed by an "ue" when conjugated in the present tense, then that same "o" is changed by an "u" in the gerund verb conjugation. This is the case with "dormir" (to sleep), which is conjugated as "duermo" in the present tense and "durmiendo" in gerund.

Regular Verb Conjugation

Once you've understood base verb forms, infinitive conjugation, and infinitive suffixes, you have all the pieces to learn Spanish regular verb conjugation. Learning Spanish regular verb conjugation is difficult for non-native Spanish speakers because Spanish verbs, unlike English verbs, adapt their conjugations to the grammatical persons and the time tenses.

Since Spanish has seventeen verb tenses, learning the verb conjugation of every single verb sounds impossible. However, luckily for us, there's a pattern to follow for every regular verb, and once you learn that pattern, you'll be able to conjugate every verb.

Most Spanish verbs are regular verbs, which makes our task of learning verb conjugation much easier.

Spanish divides verbs into three groups depending on their infinitive suffix, and each one of these groups has its own verb conjugation. Therefore, Spanish has a regular conjugation pattern for verbs that end with "ar", another one for verbs ending with "er", and a third one for verbs that end with "ir".

All that regular conjugation patterns do to a verb is take its base form and change the suffix depending on the occasion, so pay attention to these suffixes and you'll learn to conjugate any regular verbs with the same infinitive suffix. In this book, we'll use the verbs "amar" (to love), "comer" (to eat), and "vivir" (to live) as regular verbs for all of our examples of verb conjugation patterns.

We'll go over verb conjugation in the present tense in this chapter and cover the remaining verb tenses in the sixth chapter.

Verbs With "Ar" as Infinitive Suffix

All regular verbs with "ar" as infinitive will follow the same conjugation pattern as the verb "amar".

Verb Conjugation	Pronunciation	Translation	Grammatical Person
Amo	Ah-moh	Love	First person singular.
Amas	Ah-mahs	Love	Second person

			singular (informal).
Ama	Ah-mah	Love	Second person singular (formal).
Ama	Ah-mah	Loves	Third person singular.
Amamos	Ah-mah-mohs	Love	First person plural.
Amáis	Ah-mah_ees	Love	Second person plural (informal).
Aman	Ah-mahn	Love	Second person plural (formal).
Aman	Ah-mahn	Love	Third person plural.

Verbs With "Er" as Infinitive Suffix

All regular verbs with "er" as infinitive suffix will follow the same conjugation pattern as the verb "comer".

Verb Conjugation	Pronunciation	Translation	Grammatical Person
Como	Coh-moh	Eat	First person singular.
Comes	Coh-mehs	Eat	Second person singular (informal).
Come	Coh-meh	Eat	Second person singular (formal).
Come	Coh-meh	Eats	Third person singular.
Comemos	Coh-meh-mohs	Eat	First person plural.
Coméis	Coh-meh_ees	Eat	Second person plural (informal).

Comen	Coh-mehn	Eat	Second person plural (formal).
Comen	Coh-mehn	Eat	Third person plural.

Verbs With "Ir" as Infinitive Suffix

All regular verbs with "ir" as infinitive suffix will follow the conjugation pattern of the verb "vivir".

Verb Conjugation	Pronunciation	Translation	Grammatical Person
Vivo	Bee-boh	Live	First person singular.
Vives	Bee-behs	Live	Second person singular (informal).
Vive	Bee-beh	Live	Second person singular (formal).
Vive	Bee-beh	Lives	Third person

			singular.
Vivimos	Bee-bee-mohs	Live	First person plural.
Vivís	Bee-bees	Live	Second person plural (informal).
Viven	Bee-behn	Live	Second person plural (formal).
Viven	Bee-behn	Live	Third person plural.

List of Common Regular Verbs

These will be common verbs you'll find in an everyday conversation, with their pronunciation and meaning.

Verbs Ending in "Ar"

Verb	Pronunciation	Translation
Acabar	Ah-cah-bahr	To finish, to bring to an end.
Acompañar	Ah-cohm-pahn-	To bring

	neeahr	company.
Aguantar	Ah-gooahn-tahr	To hold.
Ahorrar	Ah-oh-rrahr	To save.
Alzar	Ahl-sahr	To lift.
Andar	Ahn-dahr	To walk.
Apagar	Ah-pah-gahr	To turn off.
Apuntar	Ah-poon-tahr	To take note of, to point at.
Aumentar	Ah-oo-mehn-tahr	To increase.
Ayudar	Ah-yoo-dahr	To help.
Bailar	Bah_ee-lahr	To dance.
Bajar	Bah-har	To go down, to lower, to decrease.
Besar	Beh-sahr	To kiss.
Borrar	Boh-rrahr	To erase.
Buscar	Boos-cahr	To search, to look for.
Cambiar	Cahm-beeahr	To change.
Caminar	Cah-mee-nahr	To walk.
Cantar	Cahn-tahr	To sing.

Cenar	Seh-nahr	To have dinner.
Charlar	Chahr-lahr	To speak, to talk, to chat.
Cocinar	Coh-see-nahr	To cook.
Coleccionar	Coh-lehc-seeoh-nahr	To collect.
Comprar	Cohm-prahr	To buy.
Contestar	Cohn-tehs-tahr	To answer.
Cortar	Cohr-tahr	To cut, to slice.
Cuidar	Cooee-dahr	To look out for, to take care of.
Dejar	Deh-hahr	To leave.
Dibujar	Dee-boo-hahr	To draw.
Diseñar	Dee-sehn-neeahr	To design
Encantar	Ehn-cahn-tahr	To enchant, to adore, to love.
Enseñar	Ehn-sehn-neeahr	To teach, to show.
Entregar	Ehn-treh-gahr	To deliver, to hand over, to give.
Escuchar	Ehs-coo-chahr	To listen.

Esperar	Ehs-peh-rahr	To wait.
Evitar	Eh-bee-tahr	To avoid.
Examinar	Ex-ah-mee-nahr	To examine.
Faltar	Fahl-tahr	To be missing.
Fascinar	Fahs-see-nahr	To fascinate, to adore, to love.
Funcionar	Foon-seeoh-nahr	To function, to work.
Ganar	Gah-nahr	To win, to earn.
Gastar	Gahs-tahr	To spend, to waste.
Gritar	Gree-tahr	To yell, to shout.
Guardar	Gooahr-dahr	To save, to put away.
Gustar	Goos-tahr	To like.
Hablar	Ah-blahr	To talk, to speak.
Informar	Een-fohr-mahr	To inform, to tell.
Interesar	Een-teh-reh-sahr	To have interest in, to

		interest.
Invitar	Een-bee-tahr	To invite.
Lavar	Lah-bahr	To clean, to wash.
Levantar	Leh-bahn-tahr	To rise up, to lift.
Limpiar	Leem-peeahr	To clean, to wash.
Llegar	Yeh-gahr	To arrive.
Llamar	Yah-mahr	To call.
Llevar	Yeh-bahr	To carry, to bring, to wear.
Llorar	Yoh-rahr	To cry.
Manchar	Mahn-chahr	To stain.
Mandar	Mahn-dahr	To send.
Manejar	Mah-neh-hahr	To handle, to drive.
Masticar	Mahs-tee-cahr	To chew.
Mirar	Mee-rahr	To look at, to watch.
Montar	Mohn-tahr	To set on a surface, to ride.

Molestar	Moh-lehs-tahr	To bother, to annoy, to get angry.
Navegar	Nah-beh-gahr	To navigate.
Odiar	Oh-deeahr	To hate.
Olvidar	Ohl-bee-dahr	To forget.
Ordenar	Ohr-deh-nahr	To order, to tidy up.
Organizar	Ohr-gah-nee-sahr	To organize.
Pagar	Pah-gahr	To pay for.
Participar	Pahr-tee-see-pahr	To participate, to take part of.
Pasar	Pah-sahr	To pass time, to pass on, to pass.
Patinar	Pah-tee-nahr	To skate, to slide.
Pescar	Pehs-cahr	To fish.
Pintar	Peen-tahr	To paint.
Practicar	Prahc-tee-cahr	To practice.
Preguntar	Preh-goon-tahr	To ask.
Preparar	Preh-pah-rahr	To prepare.

Verb	Pronunciation	Translation
Prestar	Prehs-tahr	To borrow, to lend.
Quitar	Kee-tahr	To remove.
Robar	Roh-bahr	To steal, to rob.
Sacar	Sah-cahr	To take out, to leave out.
Saludar	Sah-loo-dahr	To greet, to say hello to.
Terminar	Tehr-mee-nahr	To finish, to end.
Tocar	Toh-cahr	To touch, to play (music).
Tomar	Toh-mahr	To take, to drink.
Trabajar	Trah-bah-hahr	To work.
Viajar	Beeah-hahr	To travel.
Visitar	Bee-see-tahr	To visit.

Verbs Ending in "Er"

Verb	Pronunciation	Translation
Aprender	Ah-prehn-dehr	To learn.

Beber	Beh-behr	To drink.
Comer	Coh-mehr	To eat.
Comprender	Cohm-prehn-dehr	To understand, to comprehend.
Correr	Coh-rrehr	To run.
Creer	Creh-ehr	To believe.
Deber	Deh-behr	To owe, to ought to, to have duty of.
Leer	Leh-ehr	To read.
Prometer	Proh-meh-tehr	To promise.
Romper	Rohm-pehr	To break.
Vender	Behn-dehr	To sell.
Ver	Behr-	To see, to look at.

Verbs Ending in "Ir"

Verb	Pronunciation	Translation
Abatir	Ah-bah-teer	To demolish, to tumble, to depress.

Abrir	Ah-breer	To open.
Aburrir	Ah-boo-rreer	To bore.
Acudir	Ah-coo-deer	To go to, to turn to, to resort to.
Añadir	Ahn-neeah-deer	To add.
Aplaudir	Ah-plah_oo-deer	To clap.
Batir	Bah-teer	To shake.
Combatir	Cohm-bah-teer	To fight.
Compartir	Cohm-pahr-teer	To share.
Cumplir	Coom-pleer	To accomplish, to stay true to, to turn a specific number of years old.
Decidir	Deh-see-deer	To choose, to decide.
Despedir	Dehs-peh-deer	To say goodbye, to fire, to bid off.
Dividir	Dee-bee-deer	To divide, to split.

Escribir	Ehs-cree-beer	To write.
Evadir	Eh-bah-deer	To evade, to avoid.
Fingir	Feen-heer	To fake, to pretend.
Hundir	Oon-deer	To sink.
Insistir	Een-sees-teer	To insist on.
Invadir	Een-bah-deer	To invade.
Latir	Lah-teer	To beat.
Nutrir	Noo-treer	To nurture.
Omitir	Oh-mee-teer	To omit.
Partir	Pahr-teer	To leave, to depart, to start, to split, to separate.
Percibir	Pehr-see-beer	To perceive.
Permitir	Pehr-mee-teer	To allow.
Pulir	Poo-leer	To polish.
Recibir	Reh-see-beer	To receive.
Rugir	Roo-heer	To roar.
Sacudir	Sah-coo-deer	To shake.

Subir	Soo-beer	To go up.
Sufrir	Soo-freer	To suffer, to withstand.
Transcurrir	Trans-coo-rreer	To elapse, to pass.
Unir	Oo-neer	To join, to put together.
Vivir	Bee-beer	To live.

Irregular Verb Conjugation

Spanish irregular verbs are those that don't follow the conjugation patterns of the regular verbs. This makes the conjugation of these verbs unpredictable, which means it's necessary to learn the conjugation of each one of these verbs individually. We'll go over the different variations an irregular verb can go through, which separates it from a regular verb.

Vowel Irregularities

Sometimes the verbs replace a vowel in the base form when they're being conjugated. In these alterations, a vowel can either be replaced by another vowel or by two vowels forming a diphthong. Let's look at the conjugations of the verbs "cerrar" (to close), "dormir" (to sleep), and "servir" (to serve) to illustrate this.

- Cerrar: Cierro, cerramos, cierren, cerraba.

- Dormir: Duermo, dormimos, durmiera, dormía.

- Servir: Sirvo, servimos, sirviera, servía.

Consonant Irregularities

There's a changed consonant in the base form of these verbs. These consonant changes are often a c for a z. The verbs we'll use as an example are "caer" (to fall), "conocer" (to know), and "agradecer" (to thank).

- Caer: Caigo, caigamos, caemos.

- Conocer: Conozco, conozca, conocemos.

- Agradecer: Agradezco, agradezca, agradecemos.

Strong Preterite Form

These verbs have a variation in their preterite perfect conjugations. Regular verbs are considered to have a "soft preterite form", and their first person singular and third person singular conjugations in preterite perfect are acute words, as you'll see in the words "amar" and "comer":

- Amar: Amé, amó.

- Comer: Comí, comió.

They're called verbs with "soft preterite form" because they're acute in those conjugations. Those that have a "strong preterite form", the irregularity in the conjugation of these verbs, is that they're grave words in the preterite perfect first person singular and third person singular conjugations. We'll use the verbs "saber" (to know), "estar" (to be), and "decir" (to say):

- Saber: Supe, supo.
- Estar: Estuve, estuvo.
- Decir: Dije, digo.

Several Base Forms

Some verbs have completely different base forms in some conjugations. The term "verbos de raíz supletiva" is used in Spanish to describe these verbs. They're almost impossible to predict if you don't know them, so the only way is to memorize their conjugations. We're going to use the verbs "dar" (to give), "ser" (to be), "ir" (to go):

- Dar: Doy, daré, daba, dé, diera.
- Ser: Soy, fui, eres, era, seré.
- Ir: Voy, fui, vas, iba, iré, fuera.

Defective Verbs

Defective verbs lack some conjugations. These verbs don't have all conjugations. Between these verbs we have the verb "hacer" (to have), "hacer" (to do), and third person verbs. The verbs "hacer" and "tener" will be covered in this chapter, so we'll focus on third person verbs.

Third person verbs can only be conjugated in the third person. They can't be used to talk about persons. Most of these words are used to speak about natural phenomenons. We'll use the third person verbs "ocurrir" (to take place, to come up with, or to happen), and "urgir" (to urge):

- Ocurrir: Ocurre, ocurrió, ocurría, ocurrirá, ocurriría.

- Urgir: Urge, urgió, urgía, urgirá, urgiría.

Common Irregular Verbs

There's a list of common irregular verbs that's important to learn as it's likely you'll find them in everyday conversations.

Irregular Verb	Pronunciation	Translation
Aborrecer	Ah-boh-rreh-sehr	To loathe, to abhor, to hate.

Acertar	Ah-sehr-tahr	To guess.
Adherir	Ah-deh-reer	To attach, to adhere.
Adquirir	Ahd-kee-reer	To acquire.
Advertir	Ahd-behr-teer	To warn.
Agradecer	Ah-grah-deh-sehr	To thank, to be thankful for.
Almorzar	Ahl-mohr-sahr	To have lunch.
Apetecer	Ah-peh-teh-sehr	To crave.
Apostar	Ah-pohs-tahr	To bet.
Apretar	Ah-preh-tahr	To tighten.
Aprobar	Ah-proh-bahr	To approve.
Arrepentirse	Ah-rreh-pehn-teer-she	To regret.
Asentir	Ah-sehn-teer	To agree, to nod.
Atravesar	Ah-trah-beh-sahr	To pass, to pass through, to cross.
Atribuir	Ah-tree-booeer	To assign, to attribute.
Avergonzar	Ah-behr-gohn-	To shame, to

	sahr	embarrass.
Caber	Cah-behr	To fit.
Caer	Cah-ehr	To fall.
Calentar	Cah-lehn-tahr	To heat, to warm.
Cegar	Seh-gahr	To blind.
Cerrar	She-rrahr	To close.
Cocer	Coh-sehr	To cook, to stitch.
Colgar	Cohl-gahr	To hang.
Comenzar	Coh-mehn-sahr	To begin, to start.
Competir	Cohm-peh-teer	To compete.
Concebir	Cohn-seh-beer	To design, to conceive.
Concertar	Cohn-sehr-tahr	To arrange, to conclude.
Conducir	Cohn-doo-seer	To drive, to conduct.
Confesar	Cohn-feh-sahr	To confess.
Conocer	Coh-noh-sehr	To know.

Conseguir	Cohn-she-gueer	To achieve, to get, to find.
Consentir	Cohn-sehn-teer	To consent.
Consolar	Cohn-soh-lahr	To console, to comfort.
Contar	Cohn-tahr	To narrate, to tell.
Constituir	Cohns-tee-tooeer	To constitute.
Construir	Cohns-trooeer	To construct, to build.
Convertir	Cohn-behr-teer	To change, to convert.
Corregir	Coh-rreh-heer	To correct.
Costar	Cohs-tahr	To cost.
Crecer	Creh-sehr	To grow.
Defender	Deh-fehn-dehr	To defend.
Demostrar	Deh-mohs-trahr	To show, to prove.
Derretir	Deh-rreh-teer	To melt.
Desaparecer	Deh-sah-pah-reh-sehr	To disappear.
Descender	Dehs-sehn-dehr	To descend.

Desconocer	Dehs-coh-noh-sehr	To disregard, to ignore.
Desfallecer	Dehs-fah-yeh-sehr	To falter.
Despedir	Dehs-peh-deer	To say goodbye, to bid off, to fire.
Despertar	Dehs-pehr-tahr	To wake up.
Desterrar	Dehs-the-rrahr	To exile, to banish.
Destituir	Dehs-tee-tooeer	To destitute.
Digerir	Dee-heh-reer	To digest.
Discernir	Dees-sehr-neer	To discern.
Disentir	Dee-sehn-teer	To disagree, to dissent.
Disminuir	Dees-mee-nooeer	To reduce, to decrease, to make small.
Distraer	Dees-trah-her	To distract.
Distribuir	Dees-tree-booeer	To distribute, to deliver.
Divertir	Dee-behr-teer	To amuse, to have fun, to

		entertain.
Doler	Doh-lehr	To hurt, to feel pain, to provoke pain.
Dormir	Dohr-meer	To sleep.
Elegir	Eh-leh-heer	To choose.
Embellecer	Ehm-beh-yeh-sehr	To embellish, to beautify.
Embestir	Ehm-behs-teer	To tackle, to lunge.
Emparentar	Ehm-pah-rehn-tahr	To join, to relate.
Empezar	Ehm-peh-sahr	To begin, to start.
Encender	Ehn-sehn-dehr	To turn on.
Encontrar	Ehn-cohn-trahr	To find.
Enloquecer	Ehn-loh-keh-sehr	To get crazy.
Ensangretar	Ehn-sahn-greh-tahr	To bleed over.
Entender	Ehn-tehn-dehr	To understand.
Enterrar	Ehn-teh-rrahr	To bury.
Errar	Eh-rrahr	To make

		mistakes.
Excluir	Ex-clooeer	To preclude, to rule out, to exclude.
Fallecer	Fah-yeh-sehr	To perish, to die.
Florecer	Floh-reh-sehr	To flourish.
Fluir	Flooeer	To flow.
Fortalecer	Fohr-tah-leh-sehr	To strengthen.
Forzar	Fohr-sahr	To enforce, to force.
Fregar	Freh-gahr	To scrub.
Freír	Freh-eer	To fry.
Gobernar	Goh-behr-nahr	To govern, to rule.
Helar	Eh-lahr	To freeze.
Herir	Eh-reer	To hurt.
Hervir	Ehr-beer	To boil.
Huir	Ooeer	To flee.
Humedecer	Oo-meh-deh-sehr	To water, to wet.

Impedir	Eem-peh-deer	To impede.
Incluir	Een-clooeer	To include.
Influir	Een-flooeer	To influence.
Ingerir	Een-heh-reer	To ingest.
Introducir	Een-troh-doo-seer	To introduce.
Instruir	Eens-trooeer	To instruct.
Invertir	Een-behr-teer	To invest.
Jugar	Hoo-gahr	To play (games).
Llover	Yoh-behr	To rain.
Lucir	Loo-seer	To wear, to shine, to model.
Manifestar	Mah-nee-fehs-tahr	To manifest.
Medir	Meh-deer	To measure.
Mentir	Mehn-teer	To lie.
Merendar	Meh-rehn-dahr	To have a snack.
Morder	Mohr-dehr	To bite.

Morir	Moh-reer	To die.
Mostrar	Mohs-trahr	To show.
Mover	Moh-behr	To move.
Nacer	Nah-sehr	To be born.
Negar	Neh-gahr	To negate, to deny.
Obedecer	Oh-beh-deh-sehr	To obey.
Obstruir	Ohbs-trooeer	To block, to obstruct.
Ofrecer	Oh-freh-sehr	To offer.
Oler	Oh-lehr	To smell
Oscurecer	Ohs-coo-reh-sehr	To obscure
Padecer	Pah-deh-sehr	To endure, to suffer.
Parecer	Pah-reh-sehr	To appear, to seem.
Pedir	Peh-deer	To ask.
Pensar	Pehn-sahr	To think.
Perecer	Peh-reh-sehr	To perish.
Pertenecer	Pehr-teh-neh-sehr	To belong.

Perseguir	Pehr-she-gueer	To follow, to pursue.
Poder	Poh-dehr	Can
Poner	Poh-nehr	To put on, to place.
Preferir	Preh-feh-reer	To prefer.
Presentir	Preh-sehn-teer	To sense, to forebode.
Probar	Proh-bahr	To taste, to try.
Producir	Proh-doo-seer	To produce.
Querer	Keh-rehr	To care for, to love, to want.
Quebrar	Keh-brahr	To break.
Recomendar	Reh-coh-mehn-dahr	To recommend.
Reconstruír	Reh-cohns-trooeer	To reconstruct, to rebuild.
Recordar	Reh-cohr-dahr	To remember.
Reducir	Reh-doo-seer	To reduce.
Referir	Reh-feh-reer	To refer.
Regar	Reh-gahr	To water, to irrigate, to

		spread.
Reír	Reh-eer	To laugh.
Rendir	Rehn-deer	To yield, to render, to surrender, to pay.
Renovar	Reh-noh-bahr	To renovate, to renew.
Requerir	Reh-keh-reer	To require.
Repetir	Reh-peh-teer	To repeat.
Reproduce	Reh-proh-doo-seer	To reproduce.
Resolver	Reh-sohl-behr	To solve.
Retribuír	Reh-tree-booeer	To retribute.
Revertir	Reh-behr-teer	To reverse.
Rodar	Roh-dahr	To roll.
Rogar	Roh-gahr	To beg.
Saber	Sah-behr	To know.
Salir	Sah-leer	To go out, to leave.
Seducir	Seh-doo-seer	To seduce.

Seguir	She-gueer	To follow.
Sembrar	Sehm-brahr	To sow.
Sentar	Sehn-tahr	To sit.
Sentir	Sehn-teer	To feel.
Servir	Sehr-beer	To serve.
Soltar	Sohl-tahr	To let go.
Sonreír	Sohn-reh-eer	To smile.
Soñar	Sohn-neeahr	To dream.
Sugerir	Soo-heh-reer	To suggest.
Sustituír	Soos-tee-tooeer	To replace, to substitute.
Temblar	Tehm-blahr	To tremble, to shake, to quake.
Tentar	Tehn-tahr	To tempt.
Tener	Teh-nehr	To have.
Torcer	Tohr-sehr	To twist.
Traducir	Trah-doo-seer	To translate.
Traer	Trah-her	To bring.
Transferir	Trahns-feh-reer	To transfer.

Trascender	Trahs-sehn-dehr	To transcend.
Tropezar	Troh-peh-sahr	To stumble, to trip.
Valer	Bah-lehr	To avail, to cost, to value.
Venir	Beh-neer	To come.
Vestir	Behs-teer	To dress.
Volar	Boh-lahr	To fly.
Volver	Bohl-behr	To return, to go back.

Verb To Be

The Spanish equivalents of the verbs "to be" aren't as essential for the language, but they're still vital for any Spanish speaker. The equivalents for the verbs "to be" in Spanish are two different verbs and their conjugations, the verbs "ser" and "estar". While both verbs can be translated as "to be" in English, the Spanish verbs "ser" and "estar" have different definitions and uses. The verb "ser" is generally used to describe conditions, situations, and aspects of identity that are permanent.

The verb "estar", on the other hand, is used in temporal situations. The reality is not that simple, which can make it difficult to learn how to use them.

There are times when using either "ser" or "estar" can change the meaning of the sentence, so only one of the two terms is correct in these cases. The following are situations where you must use either the verb "ser" or "estar":

- "Ser" is used to speak about physical or personality traits that are permanent and inherent to the person.
- "Estar" is used to talk about disposition, mood, and temporary health conditions.
- "Ser" is used to talk about identity.
- "Estar" is used when talking about physical aspects that are subject to change.
- "Ser" is used to talk about traits such as cultural background or nationality.
- "Estar" is used to talk about marital status.
- "Ser" is used to talk about affiliations and interpersonal relationships.
- "Estar" is used to speak about the location of an object.
- "Ser" is used to talk about future locations and/or moments in which an event is going to happen.
- "Estar" is used before the prepositions "en" and "a" when they go before a day of the week, a

season, or a date, only when speaking in first person plural.

- "Ser" is used to tell the time, the date, even seasons.

- "Estar" is used to talk about temporal or current situations, right before the preposition "de".

- "Ser" is used every time passive voice is used.

- "Estar" is used to speak about the cost of things when it's followed by the preposition "a".

- "Ser" is used right after time adverbs.

- "Estar" is used to speak about how something has been produced or created.

- "Ser" is used right before the preposition "para" when it's used before intentions or objectives.

- "Ser" is used to speak about the cost of something.

- "Estar" is used in progressive time tenses right before the verb conjugated in gerund. Progressive time tenses will be covered in a future chapter.

- "Ser" is used before the preposition "de" when talking about the origin, owner, of material of an object.

- "Ser" is used to speak about the profession of someone.

Now that we've covered when to use the verbs "ser" and "estar", it's time to go over their conjugations. We'll conjugate these verbs in the present tense, "preterite indefinite" tense (equivalent to simple past tense in English), "preterite imperfect" tense (equivalent to imperfect past tense in English), and future tense. All of these time tenses will be covered in the sixth chapter of this book.

"Ser" Verb Conjugation

Present Tense

Verb Conjugation	Pronunciation	Translation	Grammatical Person
Soy	Soh_ee	Am	First person singular.
Eres	Eh-rehs	Are	Second person singular (informal).
Es	Ehs	Are	Second person singular (formal).

Es	Ehs	Is	Third person singular.
Somos	Soh-mohs	Are	First person plural.
Sois	Soh_ees	Are	Second person plural (informal).
Son	Sohn	Are	Second person plural (formal).
Son	Sohn	Are	Third person plural.

Preterite Indefinite

Verb Conjugation	Pronunciation	Translation	Grammatical Person
Fui	Fooee	Was	First person singular.
Fuiste	Fooees-teh	Were	Second person singular

			(informal).
Fue	Fooeh	Were	Second person singular (formal).
Fue	Fooeh	Was	Third person singular.
Fuimos	Fooee-mohs	Were	First person plural.
Fuisteis	Fooees-teh_ees	Were	Second person plural (informal).
Fueron	Fooeh-rohn	Were	Second person plural (formal).
Fueron	Fooeh-rohn	Were	Third person plural.

Preterite Imperfect

Verb Conjugation	Pronunciation	Translation	Grammatical Person

on

Era	Eh-rah	Was	First person singular.
Eras	Eh-rahs	Were	Second person singular (informal).
Era	Eh-rah	Were	Second person singular (formal).
Era	Eh-rah	Was	Third person singular.
Éramos	Eh-rah-mohs	Were	First person plural.
Erais	Eh-rah_ees	Were	Second person plural (informal).
Eran	Eh-rahn	Were	Second person plural (formal).
Eran	Eh-rahn	Were	Third person

			plural.

Future Tense

Verb Conjugation	Pronunciation	Translation	Grammatical Person
Seré	Seh-reh	Will be	First person singular.
Serás	Seh-ras	Will be	Second person singular (informal).
Será	Seh-rah	Will be	Second person singular (formal).
Será	Seh-rah	Will be	Third person singular.
Seremos	Seh-reh-mohs	Will be	First person plural.
Seréis	Seh-reh_ees	Will be	Second person plural (informal).

Serán	Seh-rahn	Will be	Second person plural (formal).
Serán	Seh-rahn	Will be	Third person plural.

"Estar" Verb Conjugation

Present Tense

Verb Conjugation	Pronunciation	Translation	Grammatical Person
Estoy	Ehs-toh_ee	Am	First person singular.
Estás	Ehs-tahs	Are	Second person singular (informal).
Está	Ehs-tah	Are	Second person singular (formal).
Está	Ehs-tah	Is	Third person

			singular.
Estamos	Ehs-tah-mohs	Are	First person plural.
Estáis	Ehs-tah_ees	Are	Second person plural (informal).
Están	Ehs-tahn	Are	Second person plural (formal).
Están	Ehs-tahn	Love	Third person plural.

Preterite Indefinite

Verb Conjugation	Pronunciation	Translation	Grammatical Person
Estuve	Ehs-too-beh	Was	First person singular.
Estuviste	Ehs-too-bees-teh	Were	Second person singular (informal).

Estuvo	Ehs-too-boh	Were	Second person singular (formal).
Estuvo	Ehs-too-boh	Was	Third person singular.
Estuvimos	Ehs-too-bee-mohs	Were	First person plural.
Estuvisteis	Ehs-too-bees-teh-ees	Were	Second person plural (informal).
Estuvieron	Ehs-too-bee_eh-rohn	Were	Second person plural (formal).
Estuvieron	Ehs-too-bee_eh-rohn	Were	Third person plural.

Preterite Imperfect

Verb Conjugation	**Pronunciation**	**Translation**	**Grammatical Person**

Estaba	Ehs-tah-bah	Was	First person singular.
Estabas	Ehs-tah-bahs	Were	Second person singular (informal).
Estaba	Ehs-tah-bah	Were	Second person singular (formal).
Estaba	Ehs-tah-bah	Was	Third person singular.
Estábamos	Ehs-tah-bah-mohs	Were	First person plural.
Estabais	Ehs-tah-bah_ees	Were	Second person plural (informal).
Estaban	Ehs-tah-bahn	Were	Second person plural (formal).
Estaban	Ehs-tah-bahn	Were	Third person plural.

Future Tense

Verb Conjugation	Pronunciation	Translation	Grammatical Person
Estaré	Ehs-tah-reh	Will be	First person singular.
Estarás	Ehs-tah-rahs	Will be	Second person singular (informal).
Estará	Ehs-tah-rah	Will be	Second person singular (formal).
Estará	Ehs-tah-rah	Will be	Third person singular.
Estaremos	Ehs-tah-reh-mohs	Will be	First person plural.
Estaréis	Ehs-tah-reh_ees	Will be	Second person plural (informal).
Estarán	Ehs-tah-rahn	Will be	Second person plural

			(formal).
Estarán	Ehs-tah-rahn	Will be	Third person plural.

Verb To Do

The Spanish verb "hacer" isn't used as often as its English equivalent (to do), however, it's still very relevant and widely used in everyday conversations. The verb "to do" will also be conjugated in present tense, preterite indefinite tense, preterite imperfect tense, and future tense.

Present Tense

Verb Conjugation	Pronunciation	Translation	Grammatical Person
Hago	Ah-goh	Do	First person singular.
Haces	Ah-sehs	Do	Second person singular (informal).
Hace	Ah-seh	Do	Second person singular

			(formal).
Hace	Ah-seh	Does	Third person singular.
Hacemos	Ah-seh-mohs	Do	First person plural.
Hacéis	Ah-seh_ees	Do	Second person plural (informal).
Hacen	Ah-sehn	Do	Second person plural (formal).
Hacen	Ah-sehn	Do	Third person plural.

Preterite Indefinite

Verb Conjugation	Pronunciation	Translation	Grammatical Person
Hice	Ee-seh	Did	First person singular.

Hiciste	Ee-sees-teh	Did	Second person singular (informal).
Hizo	Ee-soh	Did	Second person singular (formal).
Hizo	Ee-soh	Did	Third person singular.
Hicimos	Ee-see-mohs	Did	First person plural.
Hicisteis	Ee-sees-teh_ees	Did	Second person plural (informal).
Hicieron	Ee-see_eh-rohn	Did	Second person plural (formal).
Hicieron	Ee-see_eh-rohn	Did	Third person plural.

Preterite Imperfect

Verb Conjugation	Pronunciation	Translation	Grammatical Person
Hacía	Ah-see-ah	Did	First person singular.
Hacías	Ah-see-ahs	Did	Second person singular (informal).
Hacía	Ah-see-ah	Did	Second person singular (formal).
Hacía	Ah-see-ah	Did	Third person singular.
Hacíamos	Ah-see-ah-mohs	Did	First person plural.
Hacíais	Ah-see-ah_ees	Did	Second person plural (informal).
Hacían	Ah-see-ahn	Did	Second person plural

			(formal).
Hacían	Ah-see-ahn	Did	Third person plural.

Future Tense

Verb Conjugation	Pronunciation	Translation	Grammatical Person
Haré	Ah-reh	Will do	First person singular.
Harás	Ah-rahs	Will do	Second person singular (informal).
Hará	Ah-rah	Will do	Second person singular (formal).
Hará	Ah-rah	Will do	Third person singular.
Haremos	Ah-reh-mohs	Will do	First person plural.

Haréis	Ah-reh_ees	Will do	Second person plural (informal).
Harán	Ah-rahn	Will do	Second person plural (formal).
Harán	Ah-rahn	Will do	Third person plural.

Verb To Have

Similar to what happens with the Spanish equivalent of the verb "to be", the Spanish equivalents of the verbs "to have" are not one verb, but two different verbs. These are the verbs "haber", and the verb "tener". Out of these two verbs, the verb "tener" is used to speak about duty and ownership, while the verb "haber" speaks about the presence of objects and persons, and it also fulfills the role of the verb "to have" in complex verb tenses.

While there are plenty of situations that you can use either "tener" or "haber" with no issues, there are still plenty of situations where only one of those two verbs is correct.

- "Tener" is used when talking about possession or the contents of an object.

- "Haber" is used as an equivalent of the verb "exists" in impersonal sentences, usually preceded by a complement referencing a location, and succeded by a direct complement connecting it to the object.

- "Tener" is used to express duty or obligation in a personal voice. The formula is "tener" in an active voice + "que" + the verb in infinitive, describing the action that must be done.

- "Haber" is used in passive and impersonal voices to speak about things that must be done. The formula is "haber" in passive voice + "que" + verb in infinitive that describes the action that must be done.

- "Tener" is used to repeat or reinforce actions as an auxiliary verb, followed by a passive verb.

- "Haber" is used in complex verb tenses as an auxiliary verb, and is an equivalent to the verb "to have" in English.

- "Tener" is used to speak about age.

As we did with the previous verbs, the verbs "haber" and "tener" will also be conjugated in present tense, preterite indefinite tense, preterite imperfect tense, and future tense.

"Haber" Verb Conjugation

Present Tense

Verb Conjugation	Pronunciation	Translation	Grammatical Person
He	Eh	Have	First person singular.
Has	Ahs	Have	Second person singular (informal).
Ha	Ah	Have	Second person singular (formal).
Ha	Ah	Has	Third person singular.
Hemos	Eh-mohs	Have	First person plural.
Habéis	Ah-beh_ees	Have	Second person plural (informal).

Han	Ahn	Have	Second person plural (formal).
Han	Ahn	Have	Third person plural.

Preterite Indefinite

Verb Conjugation	Pronunciation	Translation	Grammatical Person
Hube	Oo-beh	Had	First person singular.
Hubiste	Oo-bees-teh	Had	Second person singular (informal).
Hubo	Oo-boh	Had	Second person singular (formal).
Hubo	Oo-boh	Had	Third person singular.

Hubimos	Oo-bee-mohs	Had	First person plural.
Hubisteis	Oo-bees-teh_ees	Had	Second person plural (informal).
Hubieron	Oo-bee_eh-rohn	Had	Second person plural (formal).
Hubieron	Oo-bee_eh-rohn	Had	Third person plural.

Preterite Imperfect

Verb Conjugation	Pronunciation	Translation	Grammatical Person
Había	Ah-bee-ah	Had	First person singular.
Habías	Ah-bee-ahs	Had	Second person singular (informal).
Había	Ah-bee-ah	Had	Second person

			singular (formal).
Había	Ah-bee-ah	Had	Third person singular.
Habíamos	Ah-bee-ah-mohs	Had	First person plural.
Habíais	Ah-bee-ah_ees	Had	Second person plural (informal).
Habían	Ah-bee-ahn	Had	Second person plural (formal).
Habían	Ah-bee-ahn	Had	Third person plural.

Future Tense

Verb Conjugation	Pronunciation	Translation	Grammatical Person
Habré	Ah-breh	Will have	First person singular.

Habrás	Ah-brahs	Will have	Second person singular (informal).
Habrá	Ah-brah	Will have	Second person singular (formal).
Habrá	Ah-brah	Will have	Third person singular.
Habremos	Ah-breh-mohs	Will have	First person plural.
Habréis	Ah-breh_ees	Will have	Second person plural (informal).
Habrán	Ah-brahn	Will have	Second person plural (formal).
Habrán	Ah-brahn	Will have	Third person plural.

The conjugation of the verb "haber" changes slightly in impersonal sentences. In this case, the verb will be conjugated in the third person singular of every time tense with the exception of the present tense. In the case of an impersonal sentence in the present tense, the verb is conjugated as "hay" (ah_ee).

"Tener" Verb Conjugation

Present Tense

Verb Conjugation	Pronunciation	Translation	Grammatical Person
Tengo	Tehn-goh	Have	First person singular.
Tienes	Tee_eh-nehs	Have	Second person singular (informal).
Tiene	Tee_eh-neh	Have	Second person singular (formal).
Tiene	Tee_eh-neh	Has	Third person singular.
Tenemos	Teh-neh-mohs	Have	First person plural.

Tenéis	Teh-neh_ees	Have	Second person plural (informal).
Tienen	Tee_eh-nehn	Have	Second person plural (formal).
Hacen	Ah-sehn	Do	Third person plural.

Preterite Indefinite

Verb Conjugation	Pronunciation	Translation	Grammatical Person
Tuve	Too-beh	Had	First person singular.
Tuviste	Oo-bees-teh	Had	Second person singular (informal).
Tuvo	Oo-boh	Had	Second person singular (formal).

Tuvo	Oo-boh	Had	Third person singular.
Tuvimos	Oo-bee-mohs	Had	First person plural.
Tuvisteis	Oo-bees-teh_ees	Had	Second person plural (informal).
Tuvieron	Oo-bee_eh-rohn	Had	Second person plural (formal).
Tuvieron	Oo-bee_eh-rohn	Had	Third person plural.

Preterite Imperfect

Verb Conjugation	Pronunciation	Translation	Grammatical Person
Tenía	Teh-nee-ah	Had	First person singular.
Tenías	Teh-nee-ahs	Had	Second person singular

			(informal).
Tenía	Teh-nee-ah	Had	Second person singular (formal).
Tenía	Teh-nee-ah	Had	Third person singular.
Teníamos	Teh-nee-ah-mohs	Had	First person plural.
Teníais	Teh-nee-ah_ees	Had	Second person plural (informal).
Tenían	Teh-nee-ahn	Had	Second person plural (formal).
Tenían	Teh-nee-ahn	Had	Third person plural.

Future Tense

Verb Conjugation	Pronunciation	Translation	Grammatical Person
Tendré	Tehn-dreh	Will have	First person singular.
Tendrás	Tehn-drahs	Will have	Second person singular (informal).
Tendrá	Tehn-drah	Will have	Second person singular (formal).
Tendrá	Tehn-drah	Will have	Third person singular.
Tendremos	Tehn-dreh-mohs	Will have	First person plural.
Tendréis	Tehn-dreh_ees	Will have	Second person plural (informal).
Tendrán	Tehn-drahn	Will have	Second person plural

			(formal).
Tendrán	Tehn-drahn	Will have	Third person plural.

Chapter 5: Basic Sentence Construction

In this chapter, we'll cover affirmative, negative, and interrogative sentences.

Affirmative Sentences

Affirmative sentences are used to state a fact or express an action. They're the easiest to learn in Spanish and are considered to be the baseline structure of sentences, being composed of a subject, a verb, and a complement. The subject is usually at the beginning of the sentence, but it's not impossible to place it somewhere else in the sentence. Affirmative adverbs, as well as any other type of adverbs are used, with the exception of negative adverbs, adjectives, and verbs.

El perro es grande y juguetón.

Ehl peh-rroh ehs grahnd-eh ee hoo-gueh-tohn.

The dog is big and playful.

El día está caluroso y soleado.

Ehl dee-ah ehs-tah cah-loo-roh-soh eh soh-leh-ah-doh.

The day is hot and sunny.

Placing the Complement

The complement provides information regarding the circumstances in which the action takes place. This is usually where the adverbs and any other bits of information are located, as well as adjectives depending on the sentence. Traditionally, the complement goes at the end of the sentence, but it can also be at the beginning or in the middle.

If there are many complements, location complements must be placed before time complements.

Ricardo estará en su casa al mediodía.

Ree-cahr-doh ehs-tah-rah ehn soo cah-sah ahl meh-deeoh-deeah.

Ricardo will be at his place at noon.

Complements are also organized depending on their relevance, leaving the most important ones to the end.

Jessica no fue al colegio porque está enferma.

Yehs-see-kah noh fooeh ahl coh-leh-heeoh pohr-keh ehs-tah ehn-fehr-mah.

Jessica didn't go to school because she is sick.

Placing the Verb Before the Noun

The verb is traditionally placed before the noun when the sentence starts with the complement.

Ayer jugó mi hermano.

Ah-yehr hoo-goh mee ehr-mah-noh.

My brother played yesterday.

The verb is also usually placed before the noun in passive voices.

Han caído varios jarrones en el suelo.

Han cah-ee-doh bah-reeohs hah-rroh-nehs ehn ehl sooeh-loh.

Several vases have fallen on the floor.

Negative Sentences

Spanish negative sentences are easier to learn and construct than English negative sentences. Unlike the English negative sentences, that need an auxilliary verb + not before the main verb of the sentence, Spanish negative sentences only need the negation adverb (no).

Negative Sentences on Simple Tenses

To create a Spanish negative sentence in a simple tense, all you need is to add the negation adverb before the main verb.

Ellos no juegan muy bien.

Eh-yohs noh hooeh-gahn mooee bee_ehn.

They don't play very well.

Mi familia no come carne.

Mee fah-mee-leeah noh coh-meh cahr-neh.

My family doesn't eat meat.

Negative Sentences on Compound Tenses

Compound tenses are made with an auxilliary verb (the verb "haber). For these types of tenses, the negative adverb will always go before the auxiliary verb.

Yo no he comido helado.

Yoh noh eh coh-mee-doh eh-lah-doh.

I haven't eaten ice cream.

Ella no ha venido de visita en una semana.

Eh-yah noh ah beh-nee-doh deh bee-see-tah ehn oo-nah seh-mah-nah.

She hasn't come to visit in a week.

Double Negatives

Double negatives in Spanish written with a negative adverb is optional but possible. Unlike English, Spanish allows double negatives without changing the meaning of the negation itself. These Spanish double negatives are made by combining the negation adverb "no" with another negative adverb, which we'll cover in the following diagram:

Negative Adverb	**Pronunciation**	**Translation**
Jamás	Hah-mahs	Never
Nada	Nah-dah	Nothing
Nadie	Nah-dee_eh	No one, nobody.
Ningún	Neen-goon	Neither, none.

| **Tampoco** | Tahm-poh-coh | Either, neither, nor. |

We'll cover double negative sentences with two examples, followed by an example of a negative sentence that only uses one of these negative adverbs to illustrate that they can also be used for negative sentences without double negations.

Nosotros no comimos nada de la pizza.

Noh-soh-trohs noh coh-mee-mohs nah-dah deh lah pee-sah.

We didn't eat anything of the pizza.

Ellas no vieron a nadie en el hospital.

Eh-yahs noh bee_eh-rohn ah nah-dee_eh ehn ehl ohs-pee-tahl.

They didn't see anyone at the hospital.

Yo nunca he ido a Paris.

Yoh noon-cah eh ee-doh ah pah-rees.

I've never been to Paris.

Interrogative Sentences

Since Spanish has an opening question mark (¿), it's possible to create interrogative sentences in almost any form if you don't care about being technically correct. Spanish isn't as strict as English regarding question building. You can ask a question in text, building the sentence as an affirmative sentence, and placing it between question marks to make it a question (or using a tone of voice of a querry to make the question).

However, the right way to build an interrogative sentence in Spanish is, as in English, is to start with an interrogative pronoun, interrogative adverb, or a verb. Interrogative pronouns and verbs have already been covered in previous chapters, so we'll focus on interrogative adverbs.

Interrogative Adverbs

The five interrogative adverbs are "por qué" (why), "cómo" (how), "cuánto" (how much), "dónde" (where), and "cuándo" (when). Interrogative adverbs, same as interrogative pronouns, are always written with a tilde. "Cuánto" is the only interrogative adverb that changes with the number of objects, and overall, interrogative adverbs don't change with gender.

Interrogative Adverb	Pronunciation	Translation

Por qué	Pohr keh	Why
Cómo	Coh-moh	Why
Cuánto	Cooahn-toh	How much
Dónde	Dohn-deh	Where
Cuándo	Cooahn-doh	When

We'll do an example for each one of the interrogative adverbs.

¿Por qué llegaste tarde?

Pohr keh yeh-gahs-teh tahr-deh

Because you were late?

¿Cómo limpiaste esa mancha?

Coh-moh leem-peeahs-teh eh-sah mahn-chah

How did you clean that stain?

¿Cuánto tiempo crees que nos cueste llegar?

Cooahn-toh tee_ehm-poh kreh-ehs keh nohs cooehs-teh yeh-gahr

How long do you think it'll take us to get there?

¿Dónde dejaste tu cartera?

Dohn-deh deh-hahs-teh too cahr-teh-rah

Where did you leave your wallet?

¿Cuándo vamos a ir al cine?

Cooahn-doh bah-mohs ah eer ahl see-neh

When are we going to go to the movies?

Total and Partial Interrogative Sentences

Spanish interrogative sentences are divided between total interrogative sentences and partial interrogative sentences. The only difference being that total interrogative sentences go down to the specifics; they're either yes or no questions or questions that allow multiple and yet specific answers.

Partial interrogative sentences are open questions for open answers. We'll illustrate this with a total interrogative sentence example followed by a partial interrogative sentence example, both of which will have their answers.

¿Quieres comer aquí con nosotros? / Sí, por favor.

Kee_eh-rehs coh-mehr ah-kee cohn noh-soh-trohs see pohr fah-bohr

Do you want to eat here with us? Yes please.

¿Dónde planeas ir de vacaciones? / Quiero ir a Mérida en agosto.

Dohn-deh plah-neh-ahs eer deh bah-cah-seeoh-nehs kee_eh-roh eer ah meh-ree-dah ehn ah-gohs-toh

Where are you planning to go on vacation? I want to go to Merida in August.

Indirect and Direct Interrogative Sentences

In Spanish, it's possible to ask a question without interrogative marks or the usual structure. These are interrogative sentences that are part of a compound sentence, and they're called indirect interrogative sentences.

Suppose you understand the context of what's being communicated. In that case, you'll know that it's an indirect interrogative sentence because it's a sentence asking for information without the usual tone and question marks of the usual direct interrogative sentences. You'll notice that the main sentence introduces the question, leaving space for the interrogative sentence to ask indirectly.

Besides that, indirect interrogative sentences will usually have an interrogative adverb or pronoun, and/or both sentences will usually be connected by the conjunction "si", which stands for "if". We'll illustrate this with an example of a direct interrogative sentence, followed by an indirect interrogative sentence asking the same question.

¿Por qué sigues comprando ese pan si sabes que no me gusta?

Pohr keh see-guess cohm-prahn-doh eh-seh pahn see sah-behs keh noh meh goos-tah

Why do you keep buying that bread if you know I don't like it?

Dado que sabes que no me gusta ese pan, no sé por qué lo sigues comprando.

Dah-doh keh sah-behs keh noh meh goos-tah eh-seh pahn noh seh pohr keh loh see-guess cohm-prahn-doh.

Since you know I don't like that bread, I don't know why you keep buying it.

Chapter 6: Time Tenses

Spanish time tenses are more complicated than English time tenses. There are seventeen verb tenses that are grouped under four verbal moods. We'll study the four verbal moods and the most important time tenses of the indicative mood, which is the most relevant one.

Verbal Moods

Verbal modalities or modos determine the intention of the speaker, altering the meaning of the verb and the message. Similiar to the English language, where you have indicative, imperative, and subjunctive verbal moods, Spanish has indicative, subjuntive, imperative, and conditional moods.

Indicative Mood

Almost every Spanish conversation happens in indicative mood. The four verb conjugations studied in the fourth chapter, the present tense, preterite indefinite, preterite imperfect, and future tense are all from the indicative mood. The indicative mood is used to express concrete ideas such as facts, affirmative sentences, truth statements, and information that isn't subject to be questioned.

Subjunctive Mood

The verbal modality is the subjunctive mood. Opposite the indicative mood, subjunctive mood is used to express hypotheses, hypothetical situations, possibilities, ideas, and chance.

Imperative Mood

The second most used verbal modality, the imperative mood, is used to give orders and give information. Even though it's used often, it has only one verb tense.

Conditional Mood

The conditional mood is used to express overall uncertainty in conditional situations. It has only two time tenses, and it's the less used mood out of the four verb modalities.

Indicative Tense

We'll go over the conjugations and uses of the most relevant indicative verb tenses. Out of the indicative tenses, the conjugation and uses of the indicative present tense have already been covered extensively in this book. Also, the conjugations of the preterite indefinite, preterite imperfect, and future tense of the indicative have been covered too, so we'll just study the uses of those time tenses.

Continuous Tenses

Spanish continuous tenses are constructed very similarly to the English continuous tenses. They're built with the verb "estar" as an auxiliary verb, followed by the main verb in gerund. Continuous tenses can either be past continuous if the verb "estar" is in preterite imperfect tense, present continuous if "estar" is in the present tense, and future continuous if "estar" is in the future tense.

They're used in Spanish the same way as they're used in English, to speak about events taking place (present), that were taking place during a point of reference (past), or will be taking place during a point of reference (future).

Estoy ocupado estudiando.

Ehs-toh_ee oh-coo-pah-doh ehs-too-deeahn-doh.

I'm busy studying.

Ella se estaba bañando cuando la llamé.

Eh-yah seh ehs-tah-bah bahn-neeahn-doh cooahn-doh lah yah-meh.

She was taking a bath when I called her.

Yo estaré trabajando cuando caiga la noche.

Yoh ehs-tah-reh trah-bah-han-doh cooahn-doh cah_ee-gah lah noh-cheh.

I'll be working when night falls.

Preterite Perfect

Equivalent to the English present perfect tense, preterite imperfect is composed with the auxiliary verb "haber" in present tense and the main verb in participle. This is the indicative preterite perfect tense as there's also a subjunctive preterite perfect. Regarding its use, it's the same as the use of the English present perfect.

It's used to describe situations with a clear starting and ending point that gave way to a situation relevant to the present or future or previous situations that reach the present.

Ellos han preparado la conferencia de hoy.

Eh-yohs ahn preh-pah-rah-doh lah cohn-feh-rehn-seeah deh oh_ee.

They have prepared today's conference.

No he dormido lo suficiente para entrenar hoy.

Noh eh dohr-mee-doh loh soo-fee-see_ehn-teh pah-rah ehn-treh-nahr oh_ee.

I haven't slept enough to train today.

Preterite Indefinite

It's the equivalent to the English past simple tense. It's used to describe situations with clear beginning and ending points. It's also used together with the preterite imperfect tense to describe a past situation that interrupted another past situation. The regular conjugation of the preterite indefinite tense has already been explored in the fourth chapter, so we'll go straight to some examples to illustrate its use.

Ella fue al parque el viernes pasado.

Eh-yah fooeh ahl pahr-keh ehl bee_ehr-nehs pah-sah-doh.

She went to the park last Friday.

Nosotros fuimos a la tienda buscando ropa.

Noh-soh-trohs fooee-mohs ah lah tee_ehn-dah boos-cahn-doh roh-pah ee ax-se-soh-reeohs.

We went to the store looking for clothes.

Ella solía usar esa camisa todas las semanas hasta que se manchó.

Eh-yah soh-lee-ah oo-sahr eh-sah ah-mee-sah toh-dahs lahs seh-mah-nahs ahs-tah keh seh mahn-choh.

She used to use that shirt ever week until it got stained.

Preterite Imperfect

The indicative preterite imperfect is equivalent to the English imperfect tense. It's used to describe past events that lack a clear starting or ending point. It's mostly used to describe past routines, repeated situations, repeated events, long-lasting situations with no clear beginning or end. As described previously, it's often used to describe a past action that was interrupted by another past action.

Nosotros jugábamos juntos todos los viernes.

Noh-soh-trohs hoo-gah-bah-mohs hoon-tohs toh-dohs lohs bee_ehr-nehs.

We played together every Friday.

Yo corría a diario en el parque.

Yoh coh-rree-ah ah deeah-reeoh ehn ehl pahr-keh.

I ran every day in the park.

Future Simple

The Spanish indicative future simple is equivalent to the English future simple, and it's used to describe situations that are in the certain future (or as certain as the future can be). It declares future intentions, certain predictions, and suppositions about the presents.

Si está de fiesta supongo que tendrá dinero.

See ehs-tah deh fee_ehs-tah soo-pohn-goh eh tehn-drah dee-neh-roh.

If he's partying, I guess he'll have money.

El sábado visitaré a mi abuela.

Ehl sah-bah-doh bee-see-tah-reh ah mee ah-booeh-lah

On Saturday I'll visit my grandmother.

Future Compound

Equivalent to the English future perfect tense, Spanish indicative future compound tense is used to talk about future actions or situations that must be completed before a measure of time, another future situation, or another future action. It's built with the auxiliary verb "haber" in indicative future simple and the main verb in participle.

Yo habré preparado la cena para cuando tú llegues.

Yoh ah-breh preh-pah-rah-doh lah seh-nah pah-rah ehs-teh mahr-soh.

I will have prepared dinner by the time you arrive.

Si sigues comiendo así habrás engordado para este verano.

See see-guess coh-mee_ehn-doh ah-see ah-brahs ehn-gohr-dah-doh pah-rah ehs-teh beh-rah-noh.

If you keep eating like this, you'll have gained weight by this summer.

Chapter 7: Dates and Time

In this chapter, we'll cover dates, months, seasons, and telling time.

Days of the Week

As we go over how the days of the week are pronounced in Spanish, you'll notice in the examples that the days aren't capitalized in Spanish; this is on purpose. Unlike English which capitalizes the names of the days, Spanish doesn't capitalize days and instead treats them like a common noun.

Day in Spanish	Pronunciation	Translation
lunes	Loo-nehs	Monday
martes	Mahr-tehs	Tuesday
miércoles	Mee-ehr-coh-lehs	Wednesday
jueves	Hooeh-behs	Thursday
viernes	Bee-ehr-nehs	Friday
sábado	Sah-bah-doh	Saturday
domingo	Doh-meen-goh	Sunday

Months of the Year

As with the days of the week, Spanish treats months like common nouns instead of proper nouns. This means that months aren't written with a capital letter in Spanish.

Month	Pronunciation	Translation
enero	Eh-neh-roh	January
febrero	Feh-breh-roh	February
marzo	Mahr-soh	March
abril	Ah-breel	April
mayo	Mah-yoh	May
junio	Hoo-neeoh	June
julio	Joo-leeoh	July
agosto	Ah-gohs-toh	August
septiembre	Sehp-tee_ehm-breh	September
octubre	Ohc-too-breh	October
noviembre	Noh-behm-behr	November
diciembre	Dee-see_ehm-breh	December

Moments of the Day

Just like in English, the names given to the moments of the day aren't capitalized.

Moment	Pronunciation	Translation
madrugada	Mah-droo-gah-dah	Dawn, daybreak.
mañana	Mahn-neeah-nah	Morning
mediodía	Meh-deeoh-dee-ah	Noon
tarde	Tahr-deh	Afternoon
noche	Noh-cheh	Evening, night.
medianoche	Meh-deeah-noh-cheh	Midinght.

Telling the Time

Just as in English, there's a casual way to tell the time in Spanish, and there's also military time.

Telling and Reading Casual Time

This is the most common way to tell the time in Spanish, so it's what you'll use and hear in everyday conversation. Casual time is divided into two halves of twelve hours each, AM for before noon and PM for the twelve hours after noon. The number of the hours is said first, followed by "y" (and), after which the number of the minutes is said. Once the hours and minutes have been expressed, it's possible to finish by saying "am" or "pm" depending on whether it's before noon or after noon, but it's more common to say the time of the day instead of just "am" or "pm".

3:24 PM	Tres y veinticuatro PM.
5:40 AM	Cinco y cuarenta AM.
12:10 PM	Doce y diez del mediodía.
6:33 PM	Seis y treinta y tres de la tarde.
8:37 PM	Ocho y treinta y siete de la noche.

There are some other shortcuts to tell the time, in particular the number of minutes. As in English, it's possible to say "hour and a half" in Spanish when it's 30 minutes past the hour. Also, you can say "un cuarto" and "tres cuartos" (one quarter and three quarters) when it's either 15 minutes or 45 minutes past the hour, respectively. Another shortcut for telling the time, usually restricted for minutes over forty, is telling the time by the number of minutes needed to get to the next hour. This is the Spanish equivalent for English expressions such as "five minutes until midnight", and it allows all other shortcuts such as "media" and "cuarto".

10:45 AM	Un cuarto para las once de la mañana.

2:30 PM	Las dos y media de la tarde.
3:15 AM	Las tres y cuarto de la madrugada.
8:55 PM	Cinco para las nueve de la noche.

Telling and Reading Military Time

Spanish military time is much easier but far less common. As in English military time, Spanish military time covers the 24 hours of the day as a whole from 00:00 (midnight) to 23:59 (one minute until midnight). Thanks to this, it doesn't need the terms AM or PM. The time is expressed as a cardinal number of four digits, with the thousands being the first digit of the hours, the hundreds being the second digit of the hours, and the minutes represented by the tens and the units. Before 10:00, the first digit (always a zero) is named first (cero), and then the rest of the time is told from the hundreds to the tens and units.

04:10	Las cero cuatrocientas diez horas.
22:00	Las dos mil doscientas horas.
05:43	Las cero quinientas cuarenta y tres horas.
15:31	Las mil quinientas treinta y un horas.

Chapter 8: Greetings & Simple Conversations

We'll go over some easy conversation examples so you'll better understand how to communicate easily. The grammatical context has been provided, so from this point onward, all you need is some practice reviewing simple phrases while also learning language paths and fast answers. Some of these phrases will be divided between formal and informal depending on the context and their use.

Greetings

Formal Phrases

Saludos.

Sah-loo-dohs

Greetings.

¿Cómo está?

Coh-moh ehs-tah

How are you?

Un placer conocerte.

Oon plah-sehr coh-noh-sehr-teh.

Pleased to meet you.

Formal/Informal Phrases

Hola.

Oh-lah.

Hello.

Buenos días.

Booeh-nohs dee-ahs.

Good morning.

Buenas tardes.

Booeh-nahs tahr-dehs.

Good afternoon.

Buenas noches.

Booeh-nahs noh-chehs.

Good evening / Good night.

¿Cómo estás?

Coh-moh ehs-tahs

How are you?

¿Cómo has estado?

Coh-moh ahs ehs-tah-doh

How have you been?

Informal Phrases

¿Cómo estás?

Coh-moh ehs-tahs

How are you?

¿Qué me cuentas?

Keh meh cooehn-tahs

What's up? / What can you tell me?

¿Qué hay?

Keh ah_ee

What's up?

Tiempo sin verte.

Tee_ehm-poh seen behr-teh.

Long time no see.

¿Qué tal todo?

Keh tahl toh-doh.

How's everything?

Presenting Yourself

Formal Phrases

Yo me llamo _____ ¿Y usted?

Yoh meh yah-moh ee oos-tehd

My name is _____ And you?

Formal/Informal Phrases

Mi nombre es _____.

Mee nohm-breh ehs.

My name is _____.

Yo soy _____.

Yoh soh_ee.

I am _____.

Asking Someone to Present Himself

Formal Phrases

¿Podría decirme su nombre?

Poh-dree-ah deh-seer-meh soo nohm-breh

Could you tell me your name?

¿Podría por favor presentarse?

Poh-dree-ah pohr fah-bohr preh-sehn-tahr-seh

Could you please introduce yourself?

Por favor preséntese.

Pohr fah-bohr preh-sehn-teh-seh.

Please introduce yourself.

Dinos sobre tí.

Dee-nohs soh-breh tee.

Tell us about yourself.

Formal/Informal Phrases

¿Cómo se llama?

Coh-moh seh yah-mah

What's your name?

¿Quién es usted?

Kee_ehn ehs oos-tehd

Who are you?

Informal Phrases

¿Cómo te llamas?

Coh-moh teh yah-mahs

What's your name?

¿Quién eres?

Kee_ehn eh-rehs

Who are you?

Cuéntame sobre ti.

Cooehn-tah-meh soh-breh tee.

Tell me about you.

Dime quién eres.

Dee-meh kee_ehn eh-rehs.

Tell me who you are.

Asking Someone About Themselves

¿Cuántos años tienes?

Cooahn-tohs ahn-neeohs tee_eh-nehs

How old are you?

¿Qué edad tienes?

Keh eh-dahd tee_eh-nehs

How old are you?

¿De dónde vienes?

Deh dohn-deh bee_eh-nehs

Where do you come from?

¿Dónde vives?

Dohn-deh bee-behs

Where do you live?

¿De qué te graduaste?

Deh keh teh grah-dooahs-teh

What did you graduate from?

¿Dónde estudiaste?

Dohn-deh ehs-too-deeahs-teh

Where did you study?

¿Cuál es tu profesión?

Cooahl ehs too proh-feh-seeohn

What's your profession?

¿Estás casado?

Ehs-tahs cah-sah-doh

Are you married?

¿Tienes hijos?

Tee_eh-nehs ee-hos

Do you have children?

Talking About Yourself

Yo tengo treinta años.

Yoh tehn-goh treh_een-tah ahn-neeohs deh eh-dahd.

I'm thirty years old.

Vengo de Brasil.

Behn-goh deh brah-seel.

I come from Brazil.

Vivo en Pamplona.

Bee-boh ehn pahm-ploh-nah.

I live in Pamplona.

Yo me gradué de contador.

Yoh meh grah-dooeh deh cohn-tah-dohr.

I graduated as an accountant.

Yo estudié en la Universidad de Salamanca.

Yoh ehs-too-dee_eh ehn lah oo-nee-behr-see-dahd deh sah-lah-mahn-cah.

I studied at the Salamanca University.

Yo soy un contador.

Yoh soh_ee oon cohn-tah-dohr.

I'm an accountant.

Yo trabajo como contador de una tienda de ropa.

Yoh trah-bah-hoh coh-moh cohn-tah-dohr deh oo-nah tee_ehn-dah deh roh-pah.

I work as an accountant for a clothing store.

Estoy casado.

Ehs-toh_ee cah-sah-doh.

I'm married.

Estoy soltero.

Ehs-tooee sohl-teh-roh.

I'm single.

Sí, tengo cinco hijos.

See tehn-goh seen-coh ee-hohs.

Yes, I have five children.

No, no tengo hijos.

Noh noh tehn-goh ee-hohs.

No, I don't have children.

Asking Someone About How He Is

Formal Phrases

¿Cómo está usted?

Coh-moh ehs-tah oos-tehd

How are you?

¿Cómo está?

Coh-moh ehs-tah

How are you?

Formal/Informal Phrases

¿Cómo estás?

Coh-moh ehs-tahs

How are you?

¿Cómo te encuentras?

Coh-moh teh ehn-cooehn-trahs

How are you?

¿Está todo bien?

Ehs-tah toh-doh bee_ehn

Is everything alright?

Informal Phrases

¿Te pasa algo?

Teh pah-sah ahl-goh

Is somenthing the matter?

¿Estás bien?

Ehs-tahs bee-ehn

Are you alright?

¿Cómo te va?

Coh-moh teh bah

How's it going?

¿Qué tal te ha ido?

Keh tahl teh ah ee-doh

How are you doing?

¿Qué te ocurre?

Keh teh oh-coo-rreh

What's going on with you?

Telling Someone About How You Are

Formal Phrases

Todo está bien.

Toh-doh ehs-tah bee_ehn.

Everything's good.

Estoy bien.

Ehs-toh_ee bee_ehn.

I'm good.

No estoy mal.

Noh ehs-toh_ee mahl.

I'm not bad.

Todo está mal.

Toh-doh ehs-tah mahl.

Everything is bad.

Estoy mal.

Ehs-toh_ee mahl.

I'm doing poorly.

Formal/Informal Phrases

Me va bien.

Meh bah bee_ehn

I'm doing good.

Estoy genial.

Ehs-toh_ee heh-neeahl.

I'm great.

Las cosas están mal.

Lahs coh-sahs ehs-tahn mahl.

Things are bad.

No estoy bien.

Noh ehs-toh_ee bee_ehn.

I'm not well.

Informal Phrases

Me va genial.

Meh bah heh-neeahl.

I'm doing great.

Estoy grandioso.

Ehs-toh_ee grahn-deeoh-soh.

I'm grand.

Las cosas van bien.

Lahs coh-sahs bahn bee_ehn.

Things are going well.

He estado mejor.

Eh ehs-tah-doh meh-hohr.

I've been better.

No me quejo.

Noh meh keh-hoh.

I can't complain.

He estado peor.

Eh ehs-tah-doh peh-ohr.

I've been worse.

Igual que siempre.

Ee-gooahl keh see_ehm-preh.

Same as always.

Estoy terrible.

Ehs-toh_ee teh-rree-bleh.

I'm terrible.

La estoy pasando mal.

Lah ehs-toh_ee pah-sahn-doh mahl.

I'm having a hard time.

Todo es horrible.

Toh-doh ehs oh-rree-bleh.

Everything is horrible.

Asking for Directions

Disculpe ¿Me podría indicar dónde está el baño?

Dees-cool-peh meh poh-dree-ah een-dee-cahr dohn-deh ehs-tah ehl bahn-neeoh

Excuse me, could you please tell me where the bathroom is?

¿Dónde se encuentra el patio?

Dohn-deh seh ehn-cooehn-trah ehl pah-teeoh

Where's the patio located?

Disculpe ¿Sabría usted dónde está la estación de metro más cercana?

Dees-cool-peh sah-bree-ah oos-tehd dohn-deh ehs-tah lah ehs-tah-seeohn deh meh-troh mahs sehr-cah-nah

Excuse me, would you know where the nearest subway station is?

¿Dónde puedo pedir un taxi?

Dohn-deh pooeh-doh peh-deer oon tax-ee

Where can I get a cab?

¿Dónde está el restaurante más cercano?

Dohn-deh ehs-tah ehl rehs-tah_oo-rahn-teh mahs sehr-cah-noh

Where's the nearest restaurant?

¿Dónde se ubica Santander?

Dohn-deh seh oo-bee-cah sahn-tahn-dehr

Where's Santander located?

Giving Directions

We'll go over a couple of terms in every example that are vital for giving directions. Pay attention to these terms and how they're used.

Toma el siguiente cruce a la izquierda y sigue derecho tres calles.

Toh-mah ehl see-guee-ehn-teh croo-seh ah lah ees-kee_ehr-dah ee see-gueh deh-reh-choh trehs cah-yehs.

Take the next intersection on the left and go straight for three blocks.

Avanza una calle y gira a la derecha.

Ah-bahn-sah oo-nah cah-yeh ee hee-rah ah lah deh-reh-chah.

Go down one street and turn right.

Continúa por este camino y cruza a la derecha en dos calles.

Cohn-tee-nooah pohr ehs-teh cah-mee-noh ee croo-sah ah lah deh-reh-chah ehn dohs cah-yehs.

Continue down this road and turn right in two streets.

Debes ir hacia atrás, da la vuelta en U y baja dos calles.

Deh-behs eer ah-seeah ah-trahs dah lah booehl-tah ehn oo ee bah-hah dohs cah-yehs.

You must go back, take a U turn, and go down two streets.

Asking for the Day and Time

¿Qué día es hoy?

Keh dee-ah ehs oh_ee

What day is today?

¿Qué hora es?

Keh oh-rah ehs

What time is it?

Disculpe ¿Me podría dar la hora por favor?

Dees-cool-peh meh poh-dree-ah dahr lah oh-rah pohr fah-bohr

Excuse me, could you please tell me the time?

Conclusion

Spanish becomes far easier once you learn the basics of Spanish grammar. Every concept and foundation is a step on the ladder that will give you far greater insight into how Spanish works. Now that you've completed this book, you have the basic knowledge to understand a conversation and basic Spanish text.

All that's left is for you to practice to increase your vocabulary, and that's the easiest part once you've mastered the fundamentals. Now it's time to enjoy your new language and the adventures it will bring you!

¡La mejor de las suertes para ti! (Best of luck to you!)

www.ingramcontent.com/pod-product-compliance
Lightning Source LLC
Chambersburg PA
CBHW070548010526
44118CB00012B/1265